690.89
W617   Whitney, A.
c.1
                Pads for pets

JAN 23 '80	DATE DUE		
JUL 9 80			
JUN 2 82			
NOV 17 '82			
JAN 5 83			

Pads for Pets

Pads
for Pets

How to Make Habitats and Equipment for Small Animals

ALEX WHITNEY

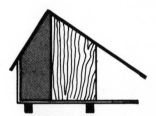

Illustrated with drawings and diagrams by Marie and Nils Ostberg

David McKay Company, Inc., New York

Library of Congress Cataloging in Publication Data

Whitney, Alex.
    Pads for pets.

    Bibliography: p.
    Includes index.
    SUMMARY: Describes how to make housing and
equipment for mammals, birds, amphibians, reptiles,
and insects which are considered fairly easy to
keep as pets.
    1. Pets—Housing—Design and construction—
Juvenile literature. 2. Pet supplies—Juvenile
literature. 3. Handicraft—Juvenile literature.
[1. Pets—Housing. 2. Pet supplies. 3. Hand-
icraft] I. Ostberg, Marie. II. Ostberg, Nils.
III. Title.
SF414.2.W47   690′.8′9   77-6106
ISBN 0-679-20426-1

10 9 8 7 6 5 4 3 2 1

Manufactured in the United States of America

Contents

Acknowledgments

The author and illustrators thank the following people for their valuable assistance in the preparation of this book:

Dr. Donald Bruning, Ornithologist, New York Zoological Park, Bronx, N.Y.; Chester E. Guthrie, D.V.M., Wilton, Conn.; Palmer Krantz, Director, Columbia Zoological Park, Columbia, S.C.; Nancy Mizener, Assistant Director, Burnett Park Zoo, Syracuse, N.Y.; Thomas C. Baer; Elizabeth Kelly; Ann Miller; The Pet Paradise, Mamaroneck, N.Y.; and The Hartsdale Pet Center, Hartsdale, N.Y.

Foreword

Owning any kind of easily kept pet—from an Aberdeen terrier to a zebra finch—can be a rewarding experience *if* the animal has proper care and harmonious living conditions.

Housing is one of the most important aspects of the art of pet-keeping. But unfortunately, many pet owners are unaware that their animals' health and development can be seriously impaired by unsuitable enclosures and the lack of exercising facilities. All too often, people place their charges in surroundings that are too damp or too dry, too bright or too dark, too cramped or too spacious, too hot or too cold. For example, most lizards thrive in relatively dry and roomy cages, while land turtles require semi-aquatic tanks with woodland atmospheres. Rabbits can adapt to the outdoors if their hutches are protected from the elements. Hamsters, on the other hand, are susceptible to cool temperatures and drafts and should be kept indoors.

If you plan to acquire a pet, or if you already own one (or it owns you), you undoubtedly hope the animal will be a healthy companion and live happily to the end of its natural life span. But in order to successfully raise and enjoy a pet, you must first be willing to learn about its characteristics and provide an environment that allows it to adjust to a life of relative confinement.

There are many valuable guides covering every phase of animal care: diet, grooming, ailments and their treatments, showing, and breeding. But we have long felt that a need exists for a book dealing solely with housing and equipment which nature would have provided had the animals remained in their natural habitats.

The following chapters describe, and show how to make, appropriate enclosures and other gear for the mammals, amphibians, reptiles, birds and insects considered to be the easiest to keep.

With the exception of equipment for free-roaming birds, we have purposely omitted habitats for wild animals because we are convinced that the best place to enjoy wildlife is in a zoo. Most wild animals require permits, and are too dangerous or too impractical to keep in the average household. But if you live in the country or in an uncrowded suburb, you can enjoy various wildlife species, such as birds, squirrels, chipmunks, raccoons and deer. The kinds of animals will depend, of course, on the area in which you live. Wild animals often welcome handouts, especially in the winter months when their food supply is scarce. If you feed them at regular intervals over a period of time, you may be able to tame them sufficiently to regard them as pets. However, once you undertake to feed them, you should continue to do so. Some wildlife species—particularly wild birds—become so dependent on you for their food that they are unable to fend for themselves if their food supply is abruptly discontinued.

We have also omitted habitats for tropical fish, principally because there are many excellent books devoted to the subject, and because the initial outlay for populating and equipping an aquarium can be extremely costly.

You don't have to be a master craftsman to build any of the projects in this book. They are comparatively easy and inexpensive to construct, and all can be made with ordinary household tools and readily obtainable materials. Since the size, or the dimensions for a few of the habitats will be influenced by the size of your pet, or if you have more than one of the same species, you can enlarge or adapt most of the projects.

At the back of the book you will find a table of common metric equivalents and conversions and a bibliography to enable you to learn further about animal care.

Pads for Pets

1

Habitats and Equipment for Mammals

DOGHOUSE

Needless to say, proper feeding, exercising and training are the basic steps in dog care. But man's best friend also needs to rest and sleep in a clean, dry place.

A house with a feeding and watering station on one side, sheltered by a roof overhang, makes an excellent outdoor living arrangement for a dog no larger than the average-sized Irish Setter, or no longer than 39″ from nose tip to the base of the tail. The ideal location for the house would be in an enclosed dog-run or a fenced-in yard. The position of the house's doorway allows the occupant to have a draft-free sleeping area. Inexpensive indoor-outdoor carpeting provides comfortable and sanitary flooring material that can be easily removed for cleaning. The raised floor of the house helps to keep its interior dry and warm in winter and cool in summer.

NOTE: The dimensions given in the following diagram can be increased to accommodate very large breeds.

CONSTRUCTION MATERIALS

2   4′ x 8′ x ¾″ pieces of exterior plywood

2   2″ x 4″ wooden studs, 35″ long

8   #8 flat-head wood screws, 1¼″ long

9   #10 flat-head wood screws, 1¾″ long

8   #8 flat-head wood screws, ⅝″ long

30   #10 flat-head wood screws, 2″ long

2   4″ angle irons

12 common nails, 1¼″ long

hand drill	screwdriver
11/64″ bit	sandpaper, medium and fine
13/64″ bit	ruler
countersinking bit	paint brush
hammer	pencil
crosscut saw	exterior paint or stain

FURNISHINGS

indoor-outdoor carpeting, approximately 3′ x 3′
   square (or 6 indoor-outdoor carpet squares)
water and food dishes

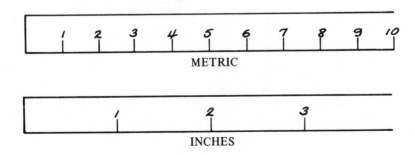

3

1. Measure and draw the layout on the two 4′ x 8′ pieces of plywood, as per the dimensions shown in Figure 1 and Figure 2. Mark each piece of plywood A, B, C, D, etc., as shown. Saw the pieces out of the plywood.

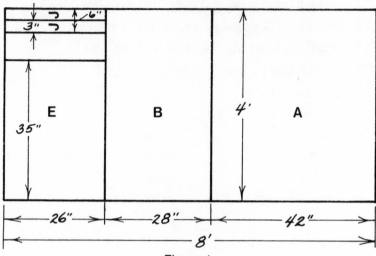

Figure 1

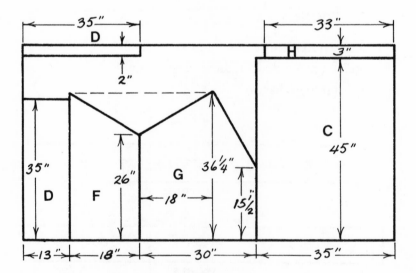

Figure 2

4

2. Measure and draw lines on the plywood piece C, according to the dimensions given in Figure 3. On each intersection of the lines, drill six holes with a 13/64″ bit. Countersink the holes, as shown in Figure 4. Screw piece C to one of the 2″ x 4″ studs with three #10 (2″ long) flat-head screws. Repeat the process with the other 2″ x 4″ stud.

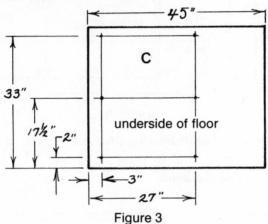

Figure 3

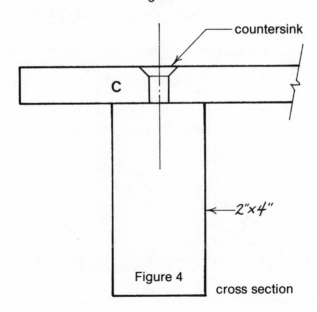

Figure 4

5

3. Turn piece C over, and measure and draw lines, according to Figure 5. Drill eight holes with 13/64″ bit. Countersink the holes.

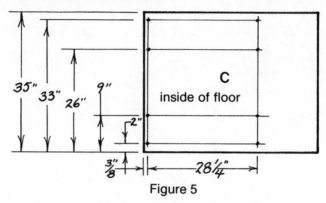

Figure 5

4. Measure and draw lines on plywood piece H, according to Figure 6. Drill eight holes with 11/64″ bit. Countersink the holes.

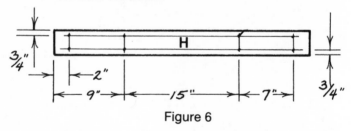

Figure 6

5. Take both sections of left side D and butt them together. Center piece H over the joint of the two

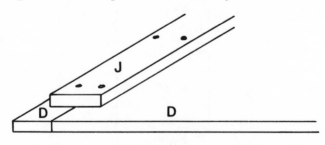

Figure 7

boards, as shown in Figure 7. Screw the boards together with eight #8 (1¼″ long) flat-head wood screws. You now have the floor and the left side of the doghouse.

6. Place the assembled floor and left side of the dog-house on end. Screw the floor to the left side D, from the bottom side of the floor, with four #10 (2″ long) flat-head wood screws. Repeat the process with right side E on the opposite side of the floor, as shown in Figure 8.

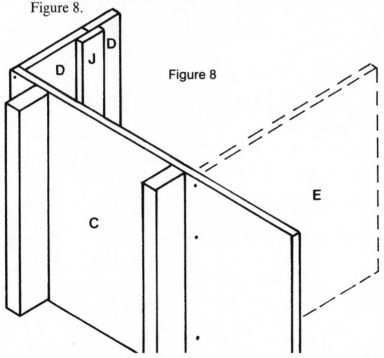

Figure 8

7. Measure and draw lines on piece F, according to Figure 9. Drill four holes with a 13/64″ bit. Counter-sink the holes. Place piece F over piece E, as shown in Figure 10. Screw piece F to pieces E and C with four #10 (2″ long) flat-head wood screws.

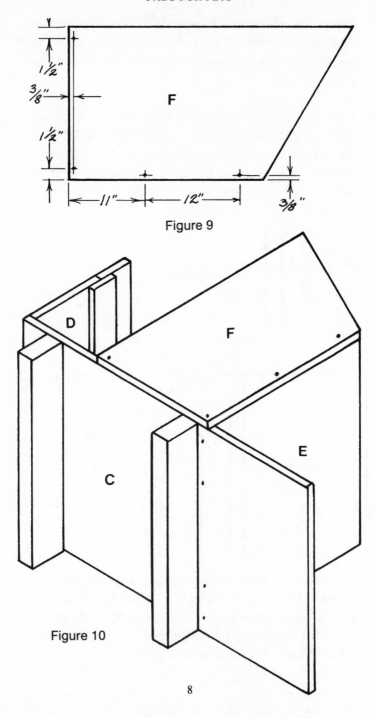

Figure 9

Figure 10

8. Measure and draw lines on piece G, according to Figure 11. Drill seven holes with a 13/64″ bit. Countersink the holes.

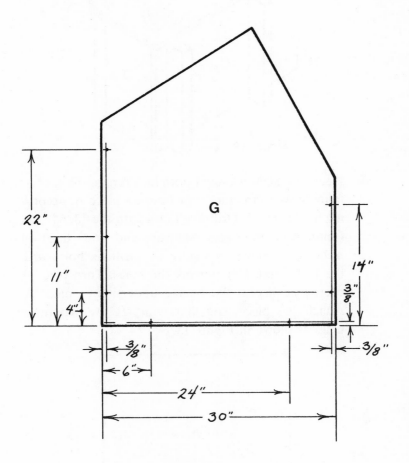

Figure 11

9. Place piece G in position, according to Figure 12. Screw piece G to pieces C and D with seven #10 (2″ long) flat-head wood screws.

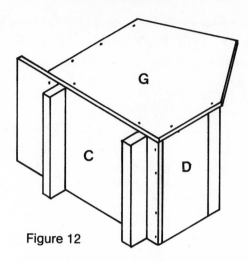

Figure 12

10. Place the doghouse shell upright. Prepare the roof as follows: Measure and draw lines on piece A, according to Figure 13. Drill five holes with the 13/64″ bit. Countersink the holes. Measure and draw lines on piece A, as shown in Figure 14. Drill six holes with the 13/64″ bit. Countersink the holes. Turn piece A over. Lay piece J flat on the underside of piece A. Attach the pieces together with six 1¼″ common nails, as shown in Figure 15.

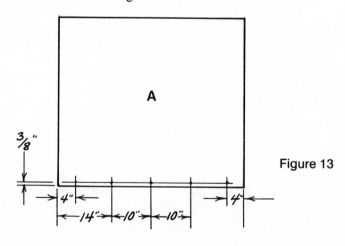

Figure 13

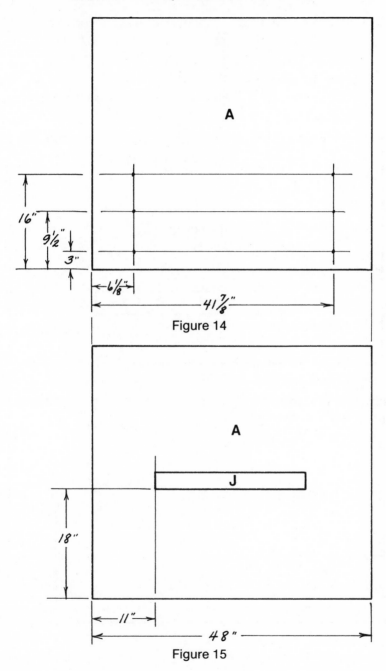

Figure 14

Figure 15

11. Measure and draw lines on piece B, according to Figure 16. Drill three holes with a 13/64″ bit. Countersink the holes. Turn piece B over. Place piece J on the underside of piece B. Attach with six 1¼″ nails, as shown in Figure 17. Position piece A so that

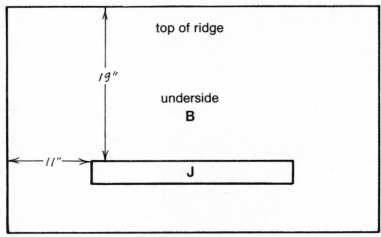

Figure 16

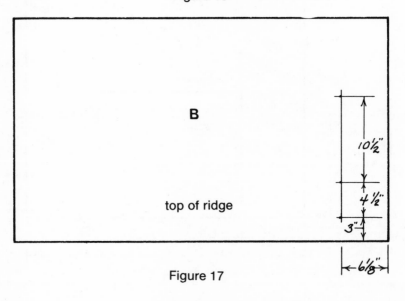

Figure 17

its underside is uppermost. Butt piece B to the edge of piece A, as shown in Figure 18. Attach pieces A and B together, using two 4″ angle irons and eight #8 (5/8″ long) flat-head wood screws. The angle irons should be placed 4″ away from the edges of pieces A and B. Turn the roof (pieces A and B) over and screw both pieces together along the top ridge with five #10 (2″ long) flat-head wood screws.

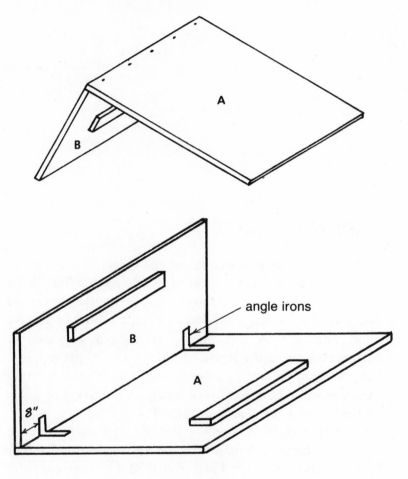

Figure 18

12. Position roof on top of the doghouse's sides and flooring. Make sure there is a 5¾" roof overhang at the front and rear of the house. Screw the roof on to the front and back pieces of the house with nine #10 (1¾" long) flat-head wood screws. Sand any rough areas of the doghouse. Then stain, varnish or paint it. Install indoor-outdoor carpeting.

PORTABLE PUP TENT

Most dogs love to travel by car and object if their owners leave them behind. If you plan to go on a day's outing or for an extended vacation, you may be faced with the problem of deciding whether to board your pet in a kennel or to take him with you. A trip with a car-trained dog can be surprisingly successful if you take along a kit of pet supplies: enough food for one or several days, a feeding dish and a water bowl, a thermos of cool water, an old towel or a dog blanket, and a portable pup tent.

Although many dogs enjoy the activities that an ocean beach, a lakefront, or other vacation areas have to offer, they often become overheated and over-tired due to an excess of unaccustomed exercise. An easily installed, collapsible tent provides a resting place, as well as a shelter from the sun or sudden showers. Its meshed entrance flap protects the dog from most kinds of bothersome insects. The dimensions given in the following diagram are suitable for dogs measuring no longer than 39″ from nose tip to the base of the tail. For very large breeds, increase the tent dimensions accordingly.

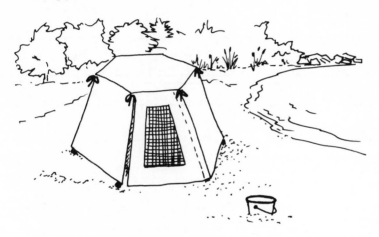

CONSTRUCTION MATERIALS

8½ yards of 45″ denim or duck fabric (solid
     color)
2′ x 2′ piece of netting
15 pieces of strong cord, each 6″ long
3   ¼″ x 1⅝″ wood lattices, 36″ long
6   1″ dowels, 36″ long
drill
5/16″ bit
machine screw 8-32 x ¾″ long
wing nut, 8-32
#8 washer

ruler	large-eye needle
tape measure	penknife
pencil	fine sandpaper
newspaper	sewing machine (optional)
pair of scissors	steam iron (optional)
straight pins	Scotch tape
heavy duty thread	

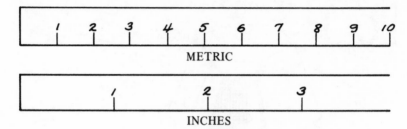

METRIC

INCHES

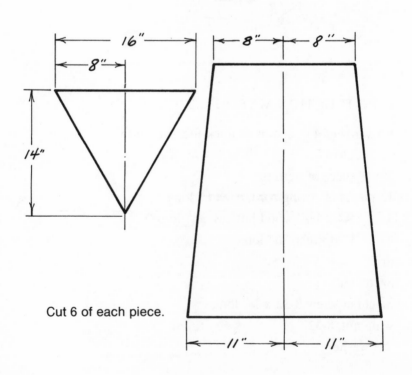

Cut 6 of each piece.

16

1. Draw patterns on newspaper and cut quantities indicated in Figure 1. Tape them together, as shown. Place patterns on fabric and cut out two pieces of each pattern.

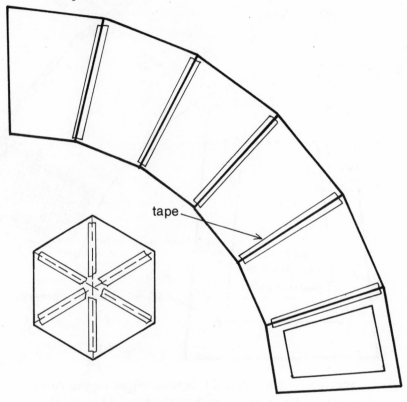

tape

fabric doubled

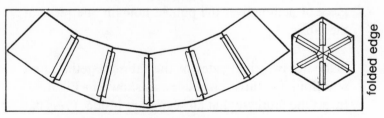

folded edge

Figure 1

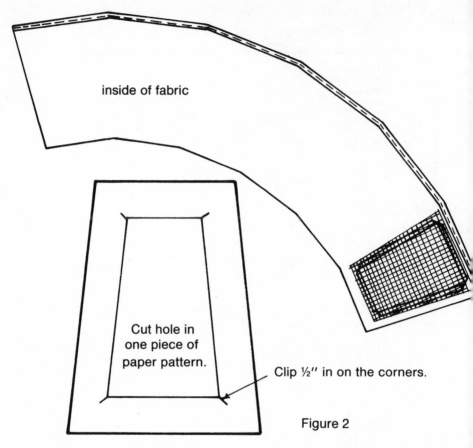

inside of fabric

Cut hole in
one piece of
paper pattern.

Clip ½″ in on the corners.

Figure 2

2. Sew a ½″ hem along the bottom edge, as shown in
   Figure 2. Pin hems on each of the two end sections of
   the fabric, and proceed according to Figure 2. Pin the
   piece of netting over the pinned hole on one piece of
   the fabric.

3. Place the two right sides of the fabric together, and
   sew along the three raw edges, as shown in Figure 3.
   Invert the fabric so that all seams are inside. Press flat
   with an iron, if necessary. Sew through all pieces of
   fabric around the net opening.

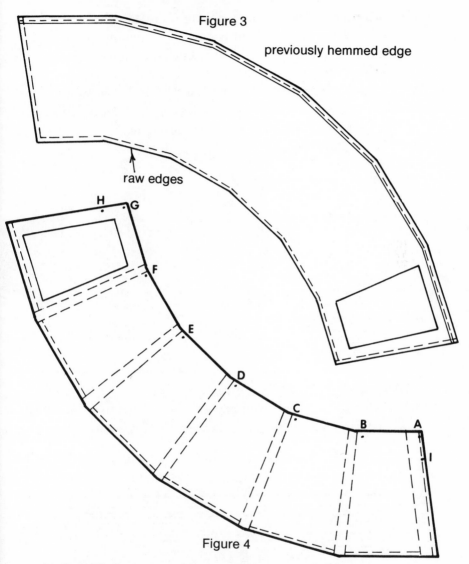

Figure 3

previously hemmed edge

raw edges

Figure 4

4. Sew 2″ slots, as shown in Figure 4. Then sew along the bottom of the fabric, leaving six 2″ slots open at the bottom. Sew five pieces of cord to points A, B, C, D, E, F and G. Sew two cords to points H and I, 3″ from the top of the fabric.

5. Place the two hexagonal pieces of fabric together and sew around the edges, leaving a 12″ opening. Turn the material inside out. Turn under the hem of the 12″ opening and sew the fabric together, as shown in Figure 5. Topstitch all around the fabric, ½″ in from its edge. Sew the 6″ cords to points A, B, C, D, E and F near the topstitching, as shown in Figure 5.

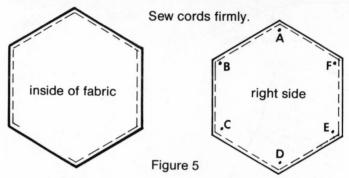

Figure 5

6. With a penknife, taper one end of each of the six 3′ long dowels.

7. Drill a 5/16″ hole in the center of each of the ¼″ x 1⅝″ x 28″ lattices. Insert an 8-32 x ¾″ machine screw and wing nut with washer, as shown in Figure 6.

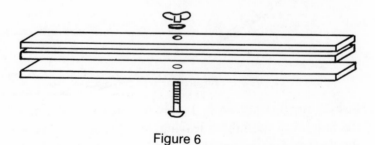

Figure 6

NOTE: In order to erect the pup tent, insert the dowels into the fabric's slots and push the dowels into the ground.

CAT'S CRADLE AND SCRATCHING POST

Other than providing food, water, litter boxes and medical care, most cat owners are faced with few concerns about the welfare of their pets. However, felines that have the run of their owners' houses often present two major problems: they like to sleep (and shed fur) on their owner's beds, and they tend to sharpen their claws on draperies, carpeting and other household furnishings.

A cat's cradle, easily taken apart for cleaning, and an attached scratching post will go a long way toward solving both sleeping and claw-sharpening problems. But your cat must be taught to use both pieces of equipment. If the animal at first refuses to have anything to do with the cradle or scratching post, attach a ball of catnip to the post as a lure. Then reward your pet with an affectionate word and a pat each time it uses the cradle and post.

The equipment should be placed in a warm spot, away from drafts and open windows. The removable canvas of the cradle should be machine washed at frequent intervals.

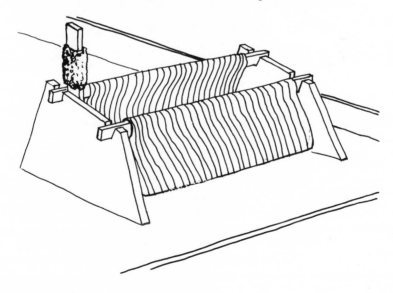

CONSTRUCTION MATERIALS

1″ x 12″ x 20″ piece of common pine wood
    (actual measurement: ¾″ x 11⅝″ x 20″)
1″ x 2″ x 5′ piece of common pine wood (actual
    measurement: ¾″ x 1⅝″ x 5′)
2   ¼″ x 7/8″ x 18″ wood lattices
6   #6 flat-head wood screws, 1¼″ long
8   finishing nails, 1½″ long
1   yard of denim, canvas or duck,
    approximately 36″ wide
carpet remnant, 4″ x 10″

screwdriver	carpet tacks
crosscut saw	pair of scissors
drill	hammer
⅛″ bit	heavy duty thread
countersink bit	large-eye needle
paint brush	pencil
paint or stain	ruler
sandpaper, medium and fine	newspaper

FURNISHINGS

catnip bag
rawhide thong, 2′ long

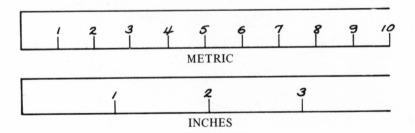

1. Measure and make a paper pattern and label it, as shown in Figure 1. Trace the pattern on to the 1″ x 12″ x 20″ piece of wood. Saw pieces A and B. Saw two slots, each ½″ x 1″, as shown in Figure 1. Drill two holes with the ⅛″ bit at the 2⅞″ and 3¾″ marks on pieces A and B. Countersink the holes.

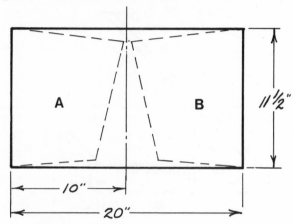

Use chisel to remove wood from slot.

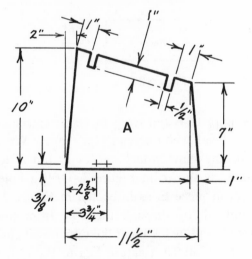

Figure 1

23

2. Saw the 1″ x 2″ x 5′ pieces of wood (C, D, E and F) into the following four lengths: 18″, 14½″, 3½″ and 16″, according to Figure 2. With a ⅛″ bit, drill one hole at each end of piece C. Countersink the holes. Screw each end of piece C to pieces D and E with two #6 (1¼″ long) flat-head wood screws.

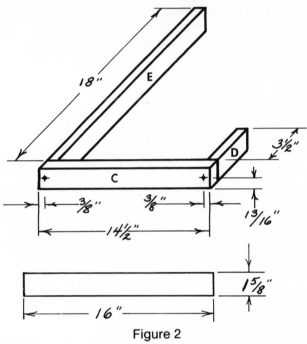

Figure 2

3. Screw piece A to piece E and screw piece B to piece D with 4 #6 flat-head wood screws (1¼″ long). With eight 1½″ finishing nails, attach pieces E and F to pieces A and B, as shown in Figure 3. Drill a hole with the ⅛″ bit in piece E, as indicated in Figure 3. Insert a rawhide thong through the hole from the outside of piece E and tie a knot at the uppermost end of the thong. Then attach a catnip bag to the other end of the thong.

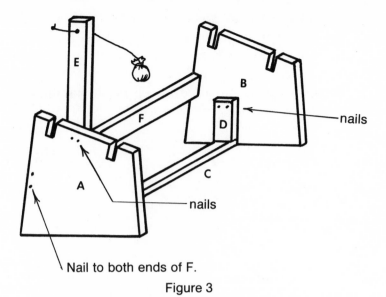

Nail to both ends of F.

Figure 3

4. Cut fabric (denim, canvas or duck) into a piece measuring 15″ x 36″. Make a 1″ hem in the fabric along the 36″ sides. Sew the two shorter ends together, inside out. Invert the fabric. Fold the fabric flat, according to Figure 4. Then sew the seams, 2″ in from each end, in order to create two slots for the insertions of the two lattice slats.

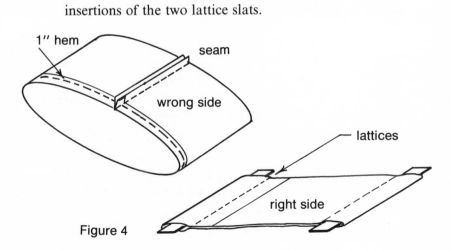

Figure 4

5. Insert the two slats into the seams of the fabric. Place the fabric and slats into the slots of pieces A and B, according to Figure 5.

6. Sandpaper all of the wood pieces. Paint or stain the wood.

7. Wrap the piece of carpet remnant around the upright piece E and tack.

RABBIT HUTCH

Many varieties of domestic rabbits make appealing and easily tamed pets that quickly adapt to life with humans. The most popular breeds are Dutch, Polish and angora. An average-sized rabbit requires a hutch measuring 18″ high, with a 3′ x 18″ floor space.

Since rabbits should be protected from dogs and other animals that prey on them, it is safer to place their hutches indoors, if at all possible. The temperature of the hutch should be between 65° and 70° F., but if warmer temperatures are unavoidable, the top and floor of the hutch can be lightly moistened with cool water. A hutch that has both sun and shade is ideal. Cover the sleeping shelf with straw or wood shavings, and replace the materials at least once a week. Place Pyrex or heavy glass water and feeding dishes in the corners of the hutch, and an enameled pan or Pyrex dish, filled with clean sand, underneath the sleeping shelf. Rabbits love to scratch and burrow in the sand. They will also appreciate a twig or a piece of wood to gnaw on and a salt block or a spool of salt.

CONSTRUCTION MATERIALS

4   2″ x 2″ x 20″ pieces of studding wood
(actual measurement: 1⅝″ x 1⅝″ x 20″)

2   2″ x 2″ x 32¾″ pieces of studding wood
(actual measurement: 1⅝″ x 1⅝″ x 32¾″)

2   2″ x 2″ x 14¾″ pieces of studding wood
(actual measurement: 1⅝″ x 1⅝″ x 14¾″)

18″ x 36″ x ¾″ piece of plywood

2   1″ x 4″ x 28¾″ pieces of common pine
wood (actual measurement: ¾″ x 3⅝″ x 28¾″)

2   1″ x 4″ x 18″ pieces of common pine wood

1″ x 8″ x 3′ piece of common pine wood (actual
    measurement: ¾″ x 7½″ x 3′)

2   2″ x 1½″ butt hinges

1½″ hook and eye

8   finishing nails, 2½″ long

4   finishing nails, 1¼″ long

8   corrugated nails, ⅜″ x 1¼″

12   #8 flat-head wood screws, 2½″ long

8   #8 flat-head wood screws, 1″ long

18″ x 13′ piece of ½″-mesh hardware cloth

2   1½″ angle irons

ruler	countersink bit
pencil	crosscut saw
hammer	wire shears
drill	screwdriver
11/64″ bit	staple gun

FURNISHINGS

salt block or spool of salt

twig or piece of wood

straw or wood shavings

sand

heavy glass or Pyrex food and water dishes

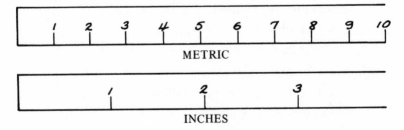

METRIC

INCHES

1. Mark dimensions shown in Figure 1 on four pieces of 2″ x 2″ x 20″ pieces of wood (A). Drill holes at marks with the 11/64″ bit. Countersink the holes.

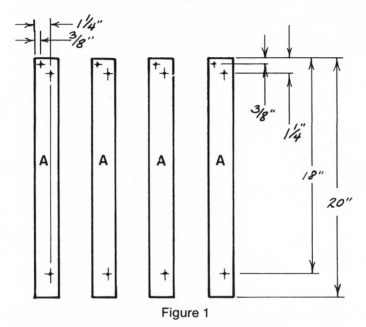

Figure 1

2. Attach pieces A to pieces B with eight #8 (2½″ long) flat-head wood screws, as shown in Figure 2.

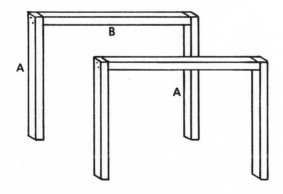

Figure 2

29

3. Nail assembled pieces A and B to piece C with eight (2½″ long) finishing nails, as shown in Figure 3.

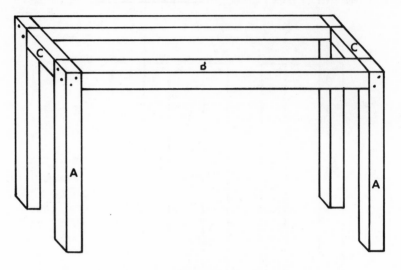

Figure 3

4. Mark and notch the 18″ x 36″ x ¾″ piece of plywood D, as indicated in Figure 4. Insert piece D between pieces A, as shown in Figure 5, and attach them together with four #8 (2½″ long) flat-head wood screws.

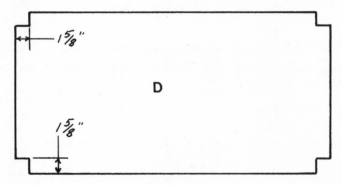

Figure 4

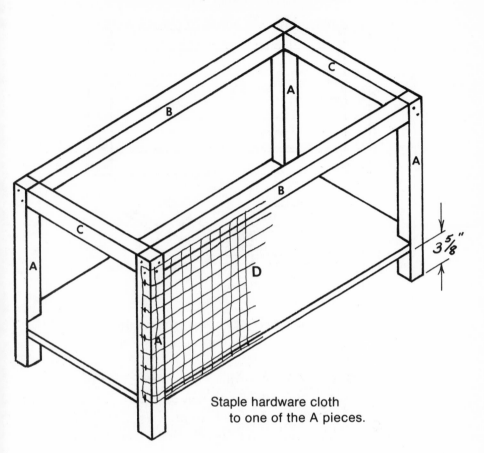

$3\frac{5}{8}''$

Staple hardware cloth
to one of the A pieces.

Figure 5

5. Using wire shears, cut hardware cloth into a 18″ x 102″ piece. Wrap it around the upper part of the hutch. Overlap the cloth on one corner of the frame and staple the cloth to the edges of the entire frame.

6. Place the two 1″ x 4″ x 28¾″ pieces of wood E and the two 1″ x 4″ x 18″ pieces of wood F on a level surface. Nail them together with two corrugated nails at each joint, as shown in Figure 6.

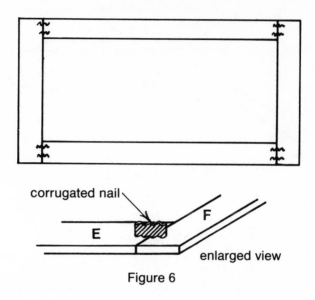

corrugated nail

E

F

enlarged view

Figure 6

7. Cut the remaining piece of hardware cloth into a 16″ x 34″ piece. Staple it to the tops of pieces E and F.

8. Place the cover on top of the hutch. Attach the two butt hinges, at the points indicated in Figure 7, with eight #8 (1″ long) flat-head wood screws. On the opposite side of the cover, install the 1½″ hook and eye.

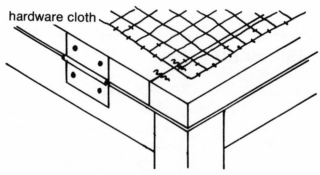

hardware cloth

Figure 7 detailed view

Center on front of piece B.

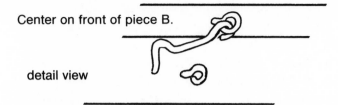

detail view

9. Saw the 1″ x 8″ x 3′ piece of wood into the following lengths: 1 piece G 16″ long; 2 pieces (H) 8″ long. Nail the three pieces together with 1¼″ finishing nails; attach 1½″ angle irons, as shown in Figure 8. Install the shelf inside the hutch.

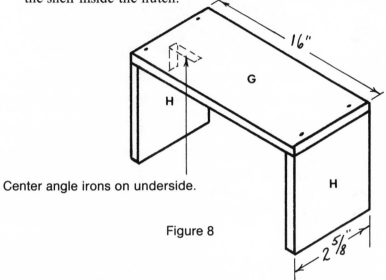

Center angle irons on underside.

Figure 8

GERBIL HABITAT

Although the Mongolian species of the friendly gerbil family are widely sold throughout the country, they are banned in some states; if gerbils were allowed to run loose and multiply, they would present a potential threat to farm crops. Be sure to check your state's agricultural laws before you invest in a pet gerbil.

Gerbils have a very sociable nature and like to live in pairs rather than singly. Their cage should be escape-proof, since gerbils are extremely lively creatures. The enclosure should never be placed in a dark corner or in cold or humid locations. The floor of their habitat should be covered with litter material, cedar shavings or sawdust. Gerbils are exceptionally clean, so you will need to clean their cage only once a month.

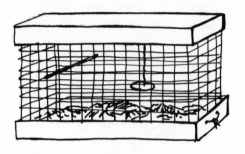

CONSTRUCTION MATERIALS

2   plastic flowerpot trays, 10″ x 20″ x 2½″
15″ x 60½″ piece of ½″-mesh hardware cloth
bendable wire, 3′ long
wire shears
drill
¼″ bit

FURNISHINGS

wooden canary perch, 10½″ long
litter or other flooring material
heavy glass or Pyrex food dish
water bottle (available at pet shops)
exercising equipment (see Gerbil Gym)
twigs or pieces of wood for gnawing

1. With ¼″ bit, drill four holes in one tray, as shown in Figure 1.

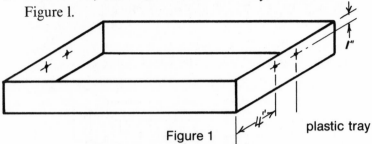

Figure 1

plastic tray

2. Place the hardware cloth on a sharp edge and bend it at 2″, 9¾″, 18½″, 9¾″, 18½″ and 2″, as shown in Figure 2.

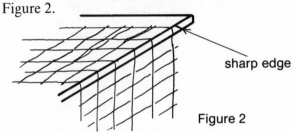

sharp edge

Figure 2

3. Lap the two 2″ creased ends of the cloth over each other. Weave the two layers together with the bendable wire and fasten securely, as shown in Figure 3. Make sure that no sharp edges protrude inside the cage.

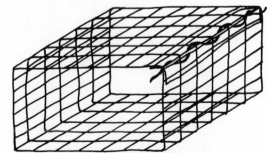

Weave together with wire and secure on both ends.

Figure 3

35

4. Place the cage (hardware cloth) upright in one of the plastic trays. Invert the other tray and place it on the top of the cage. Cut a piece of wire 6″ in length. Make a loop in the wire, as indicated in Figure 4. The loop will serve as a holder for the water bottle.

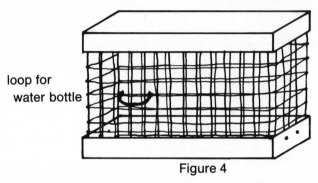

loop for water bottle

Figure 4

5. Insert wire through the holes in the bottom tray and the hardware cloth, as shown in Figure 5. Twist the ends of the wire together in order to hold the cage to its base. Repeat the process on the opposite side of the base.

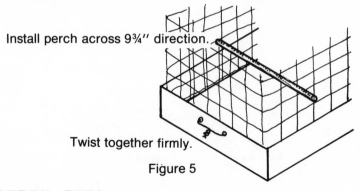

Install perch across 9¾″ direction.

Twist together firmly.

Figure 5

GERBIL GYM

SEESAW

CONSTRUCTION MATERIALS FOR SEESAW

¼″ x 1⅝″ x 9″ piece of wood lattice

36

wooden dowel, 1″ in diameter x 2″ long
#6 round-head wood screw, ¾″ long
screwdriver
fine sandpaper

1. Center the piece of wood on the dowel and screw them together, as shown in Figure 1. Sand all edges smooth.

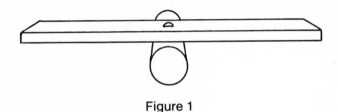

Figure 1

LADDER-TUNNEL

CONSTRUCTION MATERIALS

FOR LADDER-TUNNEL

1″ x 8″ x 9″ piece of common pine wood (actual
    measurement: ¾″ x 7½″ x 9″)
8 wooden dowels, ¼″ in diameter x 3½″ long

5½-ounce juice can,	sandpaper, medium and fine
opened at both ends	pencil
white glue	ruler
crosscut saw	penknife
coping saw	

1. Measure and mark the wood, and trace around an open end of the juice can, as shown in Figure 1. Saw

the circles in the wood, following the directions given in Figure 1.

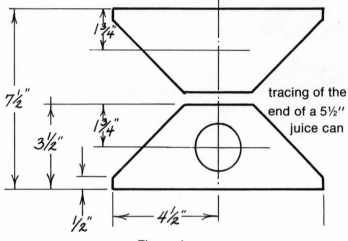

Figure 1

2. With a penknife, trim each of the eight dowels, as shown in Figure 2.

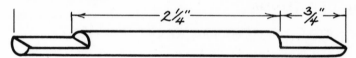

Figure 2

3. Insert the juice can through pieces A and B, as indicated in Figure 3. Stand pieces A and B upright. Using the measurements given in Figure 3, glue dowels to pieces A and B. Sand edges of wood smooth.

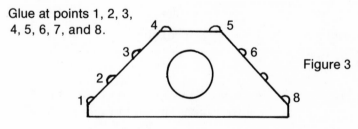

Figure 3

SWING

CONSTRUCTION MATERIALS FOR SWING

wooden canary perch, 12″ long

twine, 10½″ long

heavy cardboard circle, 2″ in diameter

1. Punch a hole in the center of the cardboard circle. Knot one end of the twine and push the knot through the hole. Make a loop with the other end of the twine.

2. To install the swing in the gerbil's habitat, push the perch through the hardware cloth. Slip the swing's twine loop over the perch, as shown in Figure 1.

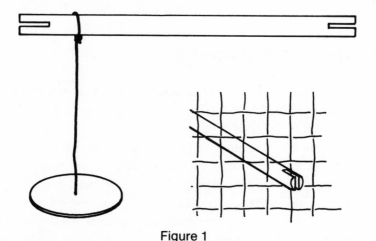

Figure 1

NOTE: The equipment for the gerbil gym is suitable for mice, hamsters and guinea pigs as well. Cardboard tubes from paper towel rolls; egg-shaped, plastic containers for pantyhose; plastic tops of used hairspray cans; and empty plastic bottles with both ends cut off also make excellent playthings for rodents.

HAMSTER HABITAT

The most familiar type of pet rodent is the golden hamster, which makes a very appealing and responsive companion. Hamsters prefer to live alone. In fact, if two or more hamsters are housed in one enclosure, they are likely to fight with one another. A hamster house should have the benefit of a small amount of direct sunlight, but it should never be placed in the open air because the breed is susceptible to temperatures below 70° F. and above 75° F. The same exercise equipment used for the gerbil gym will help hamsters to remain healthy and prevent a type of paralysis which sometimes afflicts them. The gerbil's habitat and furnishings are suitable, also, for hamsters.

GUINEA PIG HABITAT

The gentle, well-mannered guinea pig can be traced back to ancient Peru, where the breed was originally domesticated by the Incas for food, and where the animals still abound. Like hamsters and other rodents, guinea pigs need flooring materials of litter, hay or straw, and warm and well-ventilated surroundings as well. Unlike hamsters, guinea pigs like company, so it is preferable to keep more than one at a time in a cage. Although they require less exercise than other rodents, they need plenty of fresh, clean drinking water, for they are very thirsty animals.

The most suitable kind of habitat and furnishings for guinea pigs are the same as those described for gerbils. But be sure to place a salt block or a spool of salt in the guinea pigs' home.

MOUSE MANSION

Perhaps the easiest kinds of pets to keep are tiny mice—alert, fastidious and captivating creatures. The most popular breeds are the waltzing, angora, jumping and white-foot. Because of their minute size, it's advisable to keep them in their enclosures most of the time. When they are allowed to roam about, they have a habit of disappearing into nooks and crannies. A flooring of litter material or sawdust makes their habitats dry and comfortable, but the material should be replaced twice a week. Mice like to make their own sleeping nests out of the flooring plus scraps of cloth, pieces of string, and ribbons. Fresh drinking water should always be available to mice. It can be kept in an inverted water bottle fastened to the side of their cage. Since mice readily catch cold, their enclosures should be kept in dry areas with temperatures ranging between 69° and 75° F. Mice will enjoy the same seesaws, swings and other exercising equipment described for the Gerbil Gym.

CONSTRUCTION MATERIALS

clear plastic sweater box (with lid), 11″ x 16″
drill
¼″ bit
bendable wire
wire shears

FURNISHINGS

heavy glass feeding dish

water bottle (available in pet stores)

litter material

seesaw and ladder-tunnel (see Gerbil Gym)

1. Drill holes with ¼" bit in the lid of the sweater box, as indicated in Figure 1.

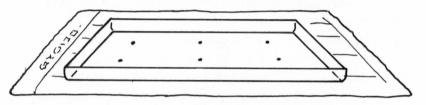

Place lid upside down on newspaper to protect the surface.

Figure 1

2. Drill three holes in locations indicated in Figure 2. Insert bendable wire for the holder of the water bottle, as shown in Figure 3. Place a 2" layer of litter material on the bottom of the box. Add a food dish, seesaw and ladder-tunnel.

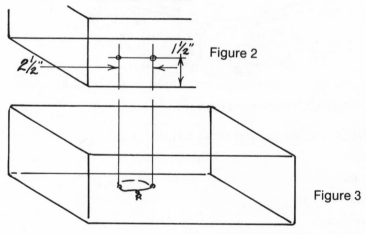

1½" Figure 2

2½"

Figure 3

2

Habitats and Equipment
for Tame Birds

CANARY CAGE

History tells us that canaries have been favorite household
pets in the Western hemisphere since 1610. More than
twenty-eight varieties have been bred in the ensuing years,
but the chopper and the roller breeds are probably the best-
known house pets. They adapt well to life in a cage if it is
located in a draft-free area with temperatures ranging
between 60° and 75° F. Most canaries like sunshine and
bathing, but too much sun during the summer months can be
harmful to them. Ready-made canary cages can, of course,
be purchased in pet shops and five-and-dime stores and

through mail-order companies. But a homemade cage, which is easy to clean and which provides shelter from drafts, is relatively easy and inexpensive to make.

NOTE: The canary cage and its furnishings are also suitable for love birds and parakeets.

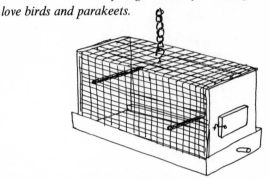

CONSTRUCTION MATERIALS

2   1″ x 10″ x 16″ pieces of common pine wood (actual measurement: ¾″ x 9½″ x 16″)

1″ x 5″ x 17½″ piece of common pine wood (actual measurement: ¾″ x 4⅝″ x 17½″)

2   ¾″ x ¾″ x 17½″ baluster moldings

½″ x 3″ x 7″ piece of clear pine wood (actual measurement: ½″ x 2½″ x 7″)

½″ x 6″ x 7″ piece of clear pine wood (actual measurement: ½″ x 5½″ x 7″)

½″ round molding, 14″ long

19″ x 52¼″ piece of ½″-mesh hardware cloth

1   plastic flowerpot tray, 10″ x 20″ x 2½″

1″ x 1″ butt hinge

1″ screw eye

8   #8 flat-head wood screws, 1¼″ long

4   #4 flat-head wood screws, ⅜″ long

2   #8 flat-head wood screws, 1½″ long

1½″ hook and eye

7   wire brads, ¾″ long

keyhole saw	11/64″ bit
crosscut saw	⅜″ bit
screwdriver	countersink bit
carpenter's square	wire shears
ruler	sandpaper, medium and fine
pencil	paint brush
staple gun	stain
drill	

FURNISHINGS

2   wooden canary perches, 10″ long

3   glass or plastic dishes for food, water and
     grit (each approximately 2″ in diameter)

cuttlebone

gravel for flooring of cage

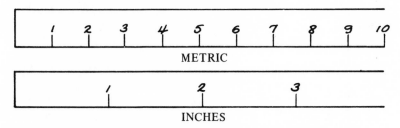

1. Measure and mark the dimensions on a 1″ x 10″ x 16″
   piece of wood A, according to Figure 1. Drill four
   holes inside the marks on each corner with a ⅜″ bit.
   Using a keyhole saw, saw along the lines drawn on
   piece A. Drill two holes in piece A with 11/64″ bit at
   points 7 and 8, and countersink the holes, as shown in
   Figure 1.

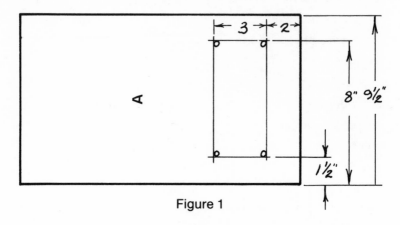

Figure 1

2. Measure and mark dimensions on the other 1″ x 10″ x 16″ piece of wood B and on piece A, according to Figure 2. Drill eight holes in pieces A and B with the 11/64″ bit at points 1, 2, 3 and 4, as shown in Figure 2. Countersink the holes. Drill two holes in pieces A and B with a ⅜″ bit at point 5.

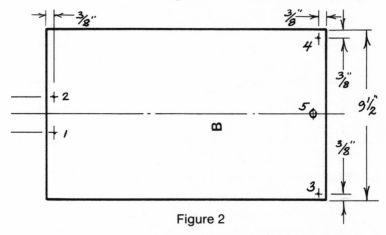

Figure 2

3. Insert 1″ x 5″ x 17½″ piece of wood C between pieces A and B. Screw them together with four #8 (1¼″ long) flat-head wood screws, as shown in Figure 3.

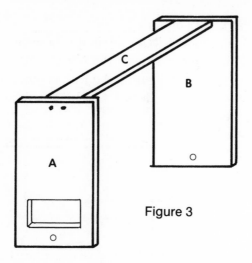

Figure 3

4. Insert two ¾" x ¾" x 17½" baluster moldings D and E between pieces A and B. Screw them together with four #8 (1¼" long) flat-head wood screws. Saw the ½" round molding into two 3" pieces and one 8" piece. Nail them to piece G with wire brads, as shown in Figure 4. Screw assembled pieces to the inside of piece A with two #8 (1½" long) flat-head wood screws.

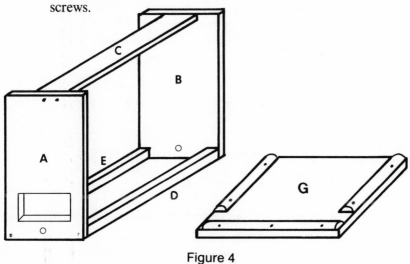

Figure 4

5. Attach the 1" x 1" butt hinge to the ½" x 6" x 7" piece of wood F with two #4 (⅜" long) flat-head wood screws. Center piece F over the outside opening in piece A, as shown in Figure 5. Attach the other side of the hinge to piece A with two #4 (⅜" long) flat-head wood screws.

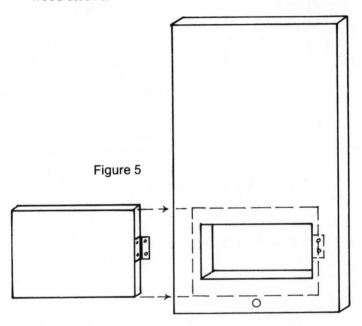

Figure 5

6. Drill two holes at each end of the plastic flowerpot tray with ⅜" bit, at the points shown in Figure 6.

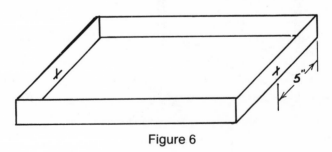

Figure 6

7. Bend the hardware cloth on a sharp edge at 2″, 9½″, 16″, 9⅝″ and 15″, as shown in Figure 7. Staple the 19″ end of the hardware cloth to piece E and the edges of pieces A and B. Continue to staple the cloth around the frame until the 15″ side of the cloth overlaps the 19″ end. Screw the 1″ screw eye into the center of piece C.

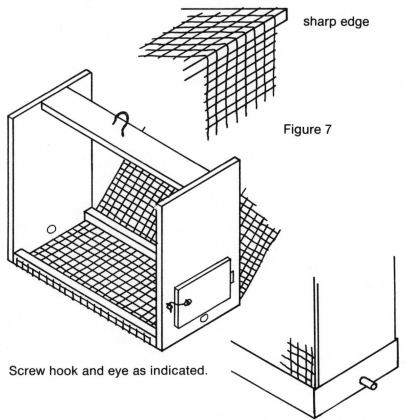

sharp edge

Figure 7

Screw hook and eye as indicated.

8. Place the cage into the plastic tray. Insert one 3″ dowel through the holes in the tray and piece A. Using the other 3″ dowel, repeat the process on the other side. Stain the wooden areas of the cage. Insert the perches.

PARROT PERCH

The parrot has ranked high as a pet ever since the days of the ancient Egyptians, Romans and Peruvians. The African gray, conure, macaw and cockatoo breeds are famed for their longevity, plumage and ability to imitate the human voice. A parrot should be frequently allowed the liberty of perching outside its cage on a stand containing a piece of rawhide on which to chew. An attached bucket, containing nuts, fruit and other treats, will help to keep the bird's attention focused on the food, rather than on household objects which parrots often take pleasure in demolishing.

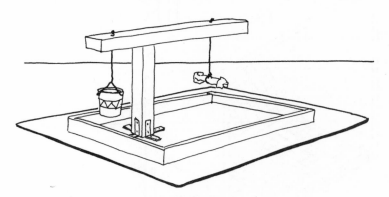

CONSTRUCTION MATERIALS

1" x 12" x 17½" piece of common pine wood
    (actual measurement: ¾" x 11½" x 17½")
¼" x 1⅜" wood lattice, 6' long

1	⅛" x 1⅛" baluster molding, 3' long
2	18" lengths of rawhide thong
4	2" angle irons
8	finishing nails, ¾" long
8	#6 flat-head wood screws, ¾" long
16	#6 flat-head wood screws, ⅝" long

2   #8 flat-head wood screws, 1¾″ long

12″ x 18″ piece of adhesive-backed felt

crosscut saw	ruler
screwdriver	pencil
hammer	paint brush
drill	stain
⅛″ bit	rawhide dog bone
¼″ bit	aluminum measuring cup
11/64″ bit	twine
pair of scissors	fine sandpaper

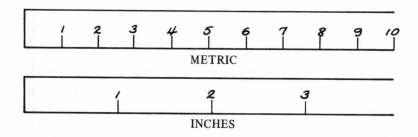

METRIC

INCHES

1. Saw the lattice into two 18″ pieces A and two 11½″ pieces B. Drill two holes with ⅛″ bit in all four pieces (8 holes), as shown in Figure 1.

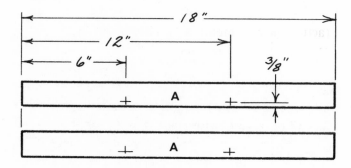

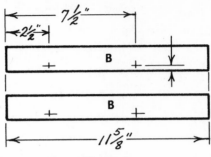

Figure 1

2. Measure and mark the 1″ x 12″ x 17½″ piece of wood C, according to the dimensions given in Figure 2.

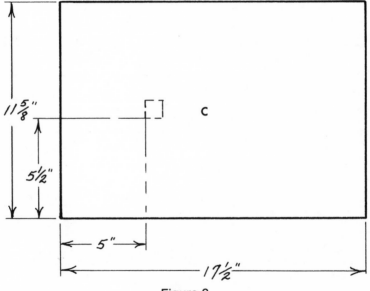

Figure 2

3. Saw the baluster molding into a 12″ piece D and a 16″ piece E. Attach four angle irons to each side of one end of piece D with eight #6 (⅝″ long) flat-head wood screws. Position piece D on top of piece C, as shown in Figure 3. Attach piece D to piece C with eight #6 (⅝″ long) flat-head wood screws.

52

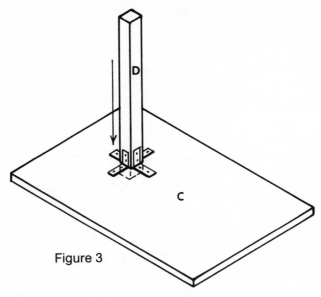

Figure 3

4. Screw pieces A and B to the sides of piece C with eight #6 (¾″ long) flat-head wood screws. Secure corners with finishing nails, as shown in Figure 4.

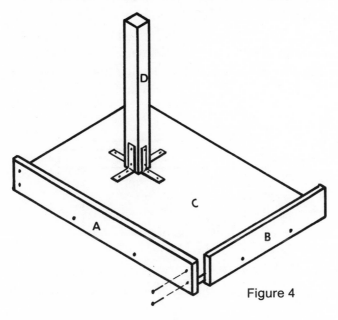

Figure 4

5. With ¼″ bit, drill two holes in piece E. Then drill another two holes in piece E with an 11/64″ bit, as shown in Figure 5.

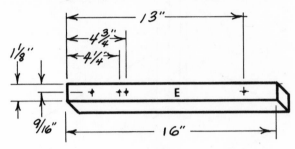

Figure 5

6. Screw piece E to piece D with two #8 (1¾″ long) flat-head wood screws. Cut the adhesive-backed felt to the dimensions of the bottom of piece C, and affix the felt to the wood. Knot one end of each length of rawhide thong. Insert the thongs through the holes in piece E, as shown in Figure 6. Drill two holes in the aluminum measuring cup with an 11/64″ bit. Knot a 6″ length of twine at one end and insert through both holes. Knot the other end of the twine. Tie one rawhide thong to the twine attached to the cup. Tie the other rawhide thong to the dog bone, as shown in Figure 7. Sandpaper the perch and then stain it.

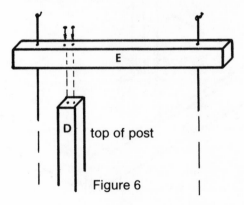

top of post

Figure 6

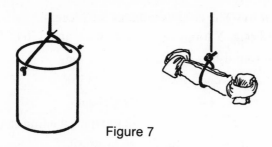

Figure 7

PARAKEET PARK

Parakeets, often referred to as shell parakeets or budgerigars, are esteemed for their wide variety of exquisite colors and for their ability to talk in brief sentences. They are a pleasure to train, and they can be allowed out of their cages for as long as an hour or so at a time, since their beaks lack the strength to do any serious damage to household furnishings. A parakeet will be healthier and happier if you provide the bird with a small exercising accommodation that can be placed on newspapers or on an aluminum cookie sheet in any draftproof area.

CONSTRUCTION MATERIALS

1" x 12" x 20" piece of common pine wood
    (actual measurement: ¾" x 11½" x 20")
1" x 2" x 18" piece of common pine wood (actual
    measurement: ¾" x 1⅝" x 18")
1   wood dowel, ⅜" in diameter x 18" long

1   wood dowel, ⅜″ in diameter x 6″ long
rawhide thong, 2′ long
1   #6 round-head wood screw, ¾″ long
2   pieces of bendable wire, each 8″ long

drill	wire shears
⅜″ bit	sandpaper, medium and fine
4 finishing nails, 1¼″ long	paint brush
crosscut saw	stain
keyhole saw	pencil
¾″ wood chisel	ruler
hammer	pair of scissors
screwdriver	newspaper
needle-nose pliers	Scotch tape

FURNISHINGS

¼″ screw eye
small bell made of heavy metal
twine
penknife
metal file

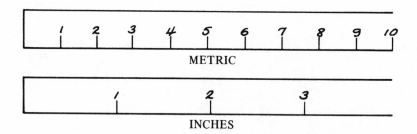

METRIC

INCHES

1. Make a paper pattern according to the dimensions
   given in Figure 1. Place it on the 1″ x 12″ x 20″ piece
   of wood and saw. Measure and label one piece of

wood A and one piece B. Saw and chisel the notches on both pieces.

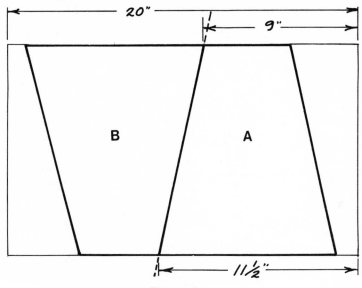

Figure 1

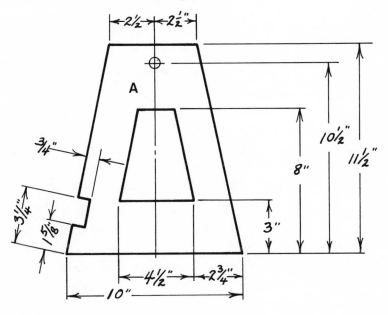

2. Drill four holes at points 1, 2, 3 and 4 on piece A with ⅜″ bit. Insert a keyhole saw into the holes and saw around the lines, as shown in Figure 2. Drill holes at points 5 and 6 on pieces A and B with ⅜″ bit.

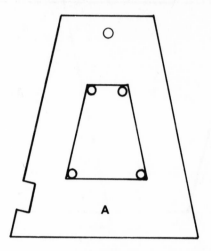

Figure 2

3. With a hammer, tap the 18″ dowel into holes 5 and 6 on pieces A and B, as shown in Figure 3.

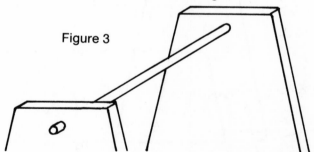

Figure 3

4. Insert the 1″ x 2″ x 18″ piece of wood C into the notches in pieces A and B. Secure with four finishing nails. Insert one #6 round-head wood screw into piece C, as shown in Figure 4. Leave ⅛″ of the screw exposed.

58

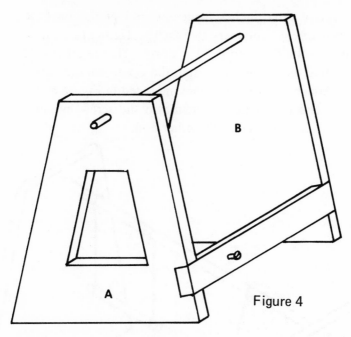

A

B

Figure 4

5. With a penknife, make two notches in the 6″ dowel, as shown in Figure 5. Tightly wind one end of 8″ wire around the notch in the dowel. Repeat the process with the other piece of wire. Make hooks on the opposite ends of the wires, as shown in Figure 5, and bend them over the 18″ dowel. Make sure the wires don't have any sharp edges.

Figure 5

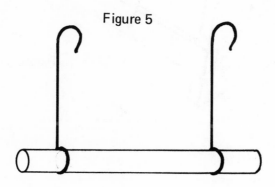

6. Starting three inches from one end of the rawhide thong, tie a knot every two inches. Tie the three-inch end of the thong to the 18″ dowel. Tie the other end around the screw. Sandpaper the wood and then stain it. Attach a screw eye where indicated in Figure 6. Tie one end of a length of twine to the screw eye and attach a small bell to the other end.

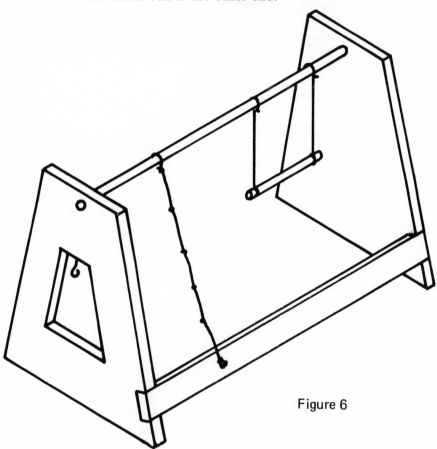

Figure 6

3

Habitats and Equipment
for Wild Pet Birds

WREN HOUSE

There are many reasons for attracting free-roaming birds to
your home site. In addition to their colors and melodic chirps
and songs, they offer an opportunity to observe wildlife
behavior at close range. And they become, in a sense, pets
that are free to live their natural lives. If you erect a
birdhouse on your grounds, your most likely tenants will be
house wrens. Of all native birds, they are the easiest to
attract. Wrens prefer a home mounted on a post five to ten
feet high. It would be wise to place squirrel guards on the
post in order to discourage animals that prey on the eggs and
young of wrens. Ideally, the front of the wren house should

have southern exposure and face away from prevailing winds. Wrens look for "unfurnished rooms," since they supply their own nesting materials.

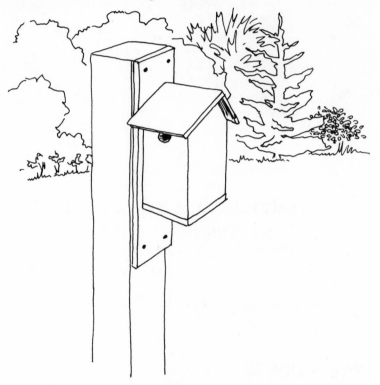

CONSTRUCTION MATERIALS

1″ x 6″ x 16″ piece of common pine wood (actual
    measurement: ¾″ x 5⅝″ x 16″)
½″ x 6″ x 9½″ piece of clear pine wood (actual
    measurement: ½″ x 5½″ x 9½″)
½″ x 6″ x 8″ piece of clear pine wood (actual
    measurement: ½″ x 5½″ x 8″)
½″ x 6″ x 7″ piece of clear pine wood (actual
    measurement: ½″ x 5½″ x 7″)

½″ x 6″ x 6″ piece of clear pine wood (actual
    measurement: ½″ x 5½″ x 6″)

½″ x 6″ x 4″ piece of clear pine wood (actual
    measurement: ½″ x 5½″ x 4″)

1″ x 5″ x 5″ piece of common pine wood (actual
    measurement: ¾″ x 4⅝″ x 5″)

4″ x 4″ x 12′ post

1″ hardware hook and eye

1½″ x 1″ butt hinge

9   #8 flat-head wood screws, 1″ long

9   #8 flat-head wood screws, 1⅛″ long

4   #4 flat-head wood screws, ⅜″ long

4   #14 round-head wood screws, 2½″ long

screwdriver	11/64″ bit
crosscut saw	countersink bit
carpenter's square	1″ bit
ruler	paint brush
pencil	stain (gray, green or earth tones)
drill	

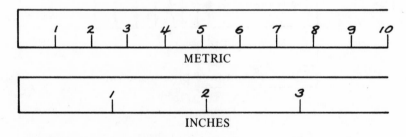

METRIC

INCHES

1. On the 1″ x 6″ x 16″ piece of wood C, measure and
mark the dimensions, as shown in Figure 1. Drill
holes with 11/64″ bit at each line intersection. On the
other side of the wood, countersink the holes marked
1, 2, 3, 4, 5, 6, 7 and 8.

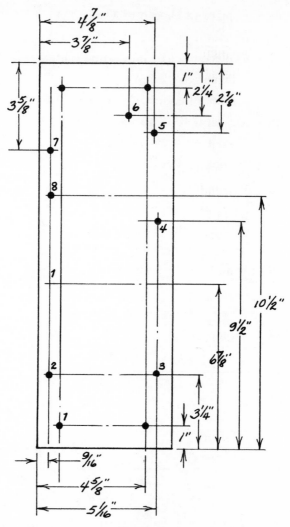

Figure 1

2. Saw front B from the ½" x 6" x 9½" piece of wood, as shown in Figure 2. Measure and mark the dimensions given in Figure 2. Drill holes with 11/64" bit at each line intersection. Countersink holes 9, 10, 11 and 12, as shown in Figure 2.

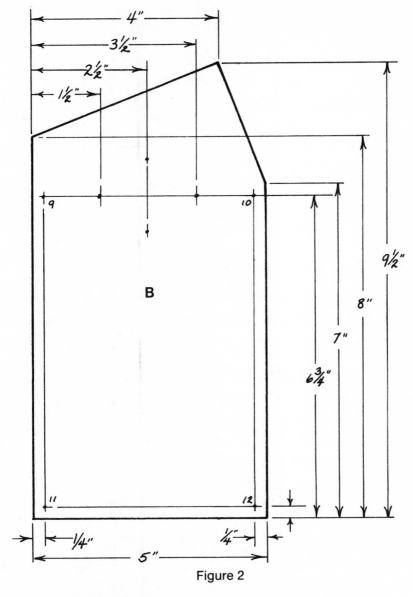

Figure 2

3. Saw right side A from ½″ x 6″ x 8″ piece of wood, as shown in Figure 3. Drill a hole with 1″ bit, according to Figure 3.

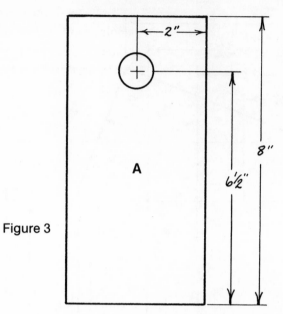

Figure 3

4. Saw left side F from the ½″ x 6″ x 7″ piece of wood, according to the dimensions given in Figure 4.

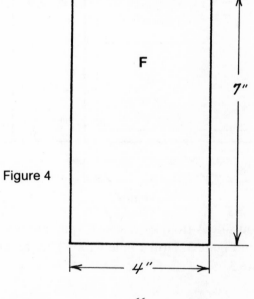

Figure 4

5. Measure and mark the ½″ x 6″ x 6″ piece of wood D, as shown in Figure 5. Drill holes with 11/64″ bit at each line intersection. Countersink the holes. Attach piece D to the ½″ x 6″ x 4″ piece of wood E with two #8 (1″ long) flat-head wood screws, as shown in Figure 6.

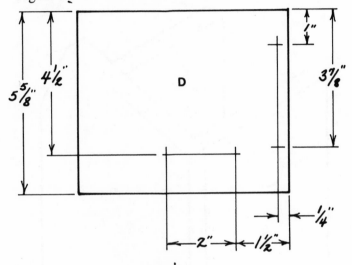

Figure 5

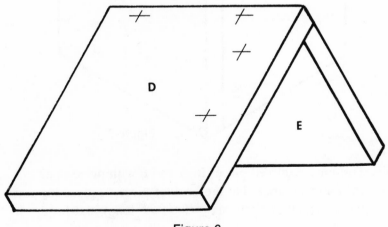

Figure 6

67

6. Place piece B on pieces A and F, as shown in Figure 7. Screw B to A and F with four #8 (1″ long) flat-head wood screws. Place assembled pieces D and E on top of assembled pieces B, A and F and attach together with three #8 (1″ long) flat-head wood screws.

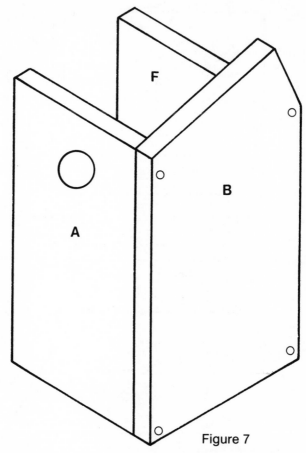

Figure 7

7. Position assembled pieces B, A and F with piece C, as shown in Figure 8. On the back of piece C, place the pieces together with six #8 (1⅛″ long) flat-head wood screws.

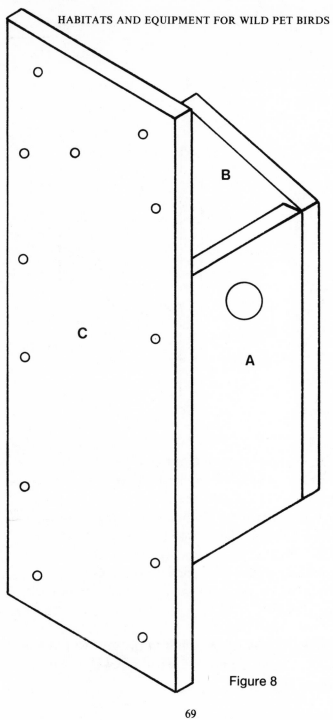

Figure 8

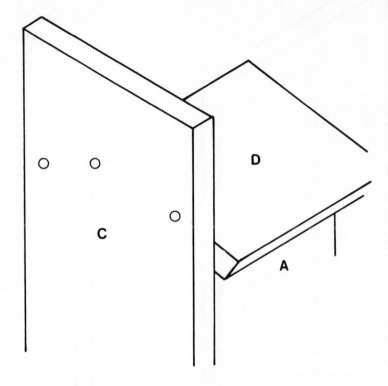

Figure 9

8. Also on the back of piece C, screw C to pieces D and
   E with three #8 (1⅛" long) flat-head wood screws, as
   shown in Figure 9. Center the 1½" x 1" butt hinge on
   piece G and attach the bottom of the hinge with two
   #4 (⅜" long) flat-head wood screws. Repeat the
   process with the top section of the hinge. On the
   opposite side of piece G, attach the screw eye to piece
   G. Then attach the hook to piece F, as shown in
   Figure 10.

9. Stain the wren house. Attach it to the post with four
   #14 (2½" long) round-head wood screws, as shown
   in Figure 11.

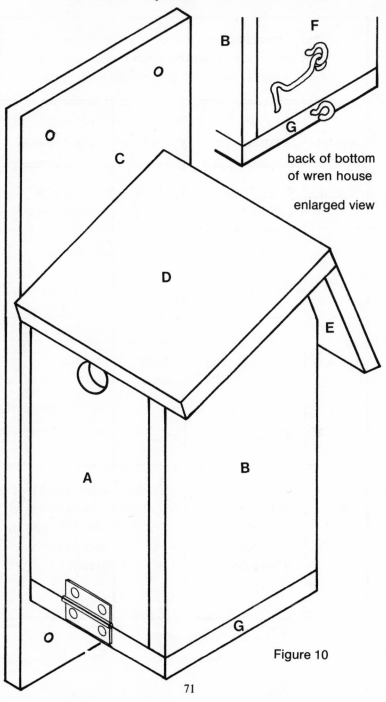

B

F

G

back of bottom
of wren house

enlarged view

C

D

E

A

B

G

O

O

O

O

Figure 10

SPECIES	HOUSE DIMENSIONS	COLORS	PREFERRED LOCATIONS
	By using this chart and the same basic design and instructions for making the wren house, you can construct houses for other varieties of wild birds.		
chickadee	5″ x 5″ base x 8″ high; entrance hole 1⅛″ in diameter, centered 6″ above floor	earth tones	area with large trees
tree swallow	5″ x 5″ base x 6″ high; entrance hole 1½″ in diameter, centered 4″ above floor	gray or earth tones	area near pond or lake
house finch	6″ x 6″ x 6″; entrance hole 2″ in diameter, centered 4½″ above floor	earth tones	open areas (species common in the West and in some eastern states)

bluebird	5" x 5" base x 8" high; entrance hole 1½" in diameter, centered 6" above floor	earth tones	near fields or other open areas
tufted titmouse	4" x 4" base x 8" high; entrance hole 1¼" in diameter, centered 6" above floor	earth tones	in or near wooded areas
robin, barn swallow, phoebe	6" x 6" base x 8" high; entrance hole 1⅛" in diameter, centered 6" above floor (Extend roof 3" over entrance side for protection against elements.)	unpainted wood	open areas near water

FEEDING STATION FOR FREE-ROAMING BIRDS

City dwellers—as well as those who live in the country or suburbs—can attract wild birds by attaching a feeding station to a window sill, terrace or balcony. The station should be placed at least eight feet above the ground, or high enough to discourage unwelcome marauders—rodents and cats, for example.

Among the many species which patronize feeding stations are sparrows, wrens, finches, grosbeaks, juncos, crossbills, nuthatches, pigeons, doves, chickadees, woodpeckers and grackles. The kinds of birds will depend, of course, on the location of the station. But once you provide food for wild birds, it is your responsibility to continue doing so, especially during the winter months when insects are scarce. Most birds that might have migrated, had they not been lured with handouts, are unable to forage for themselves if their food source should be suddenly terminated.

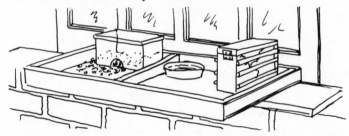

CONSTRUCTION MATERIALS

14" x 24" x ¾" piece of plywood

2   ½" x 2" x 25" pieces of clear pine wood
(actual measurement: ½" x 1½" x 25")

2   ½" x 2" x 14" pieces of clear pine wood
(actual measurement: ½" x 1½" x 14")

1   ¾" x ¾" baluster molding, 14" long

6   ⅜" wood dowels, 5" long

½" x 3" x 36" piece of clear pine wood (actual
    measurement: ½" x 2½" x 36")

2   #8 flat-head wood screws, ¾" long

32 finishing nails, 1" long

8   finishing nails, 1¼" long

6   ⅝" wire brads

1" x 1" butt hinge

2   #8 flat-head wood screws, ⅝" long

4   #6 flat-head wood screws, ½" long

1   #8 round-head wood screw, ¾" long

1½" hook and eye

crosscut saw   carpenter's square

pencil   drill

ruler   11/64" bit

hammer   countersink bit

penknife   paint brush

screwdriver   stain (earth tones)

FURNISHINGS

clay flowerpot saucer, 6" in diameter

3-quart rectangular food container (soft plastic)

suet, fruit or nuts

birdseed

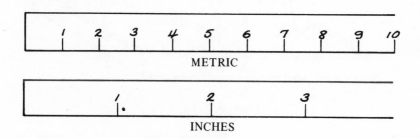

METRIC

INCHES

1. Attach the two ½″ x 2″ x 25″ pieces of wood B and the two ½″ x 2″ x 14″ pieces of wood C to the 14″ x 24″ x ¾″ piece of plywood A with thirty-two 1″ finishing nails, according to Figure 1. Measure and

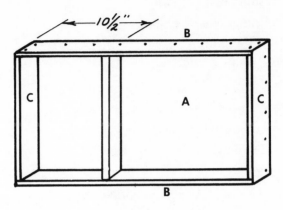

Figure 1

mark on piece A, according to dimensions given in Figure 2. Nail the 14″ baluster molding, piece G, to piece B with four 1¼″ finishing nails. Turn the assembled pieces upside-down. On the bottom of piece A, hammer four 1¼″ finishing nails where indicated in Figure 2.

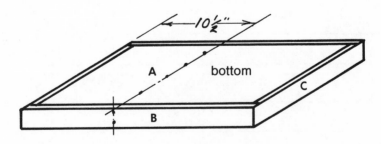

Nail both sides with 1″ finishing nails.

Figure 2

2. Cut a hole in the plastic food container, as shown in Figure 3. Punch two small holes in the center of the bottom of the container. Insert two #8 (⅝″ long) flat-head wood screws through the holes and into piece A.

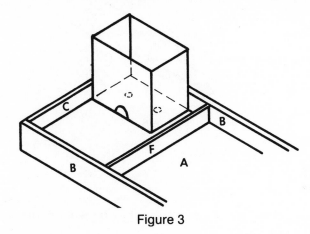

Figure 3

3. Saw the ½″ x 3″ x 36″ piece of wood into the following lengths: two 6″ pieces D, one 6″ piece E and one 7″ piece F. With wire brads, nail pieces D to both ends of piece E, as shown in Figure 4. Drill a hole in the center of piece E with an 11/64″ bit.

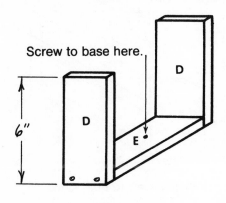

Figure 4

4. With a penknife, notch the ends of each of the six dowels, as shown in Figure 5.

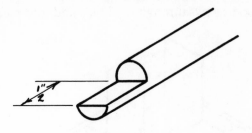

Figure 5

5. Attach the dowels to pieces D with wire brads, as shown in Figure 6.

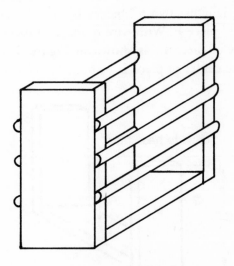

Nail dowels to both sides.

Figure 6

6. Screw the butt hinge into one end of the ½″ x 3″ x 7″ piece F with two #6 (½″ long) flat-head wood screws. Screw the other part of the hinge to piece D, as shown in Figure 7.

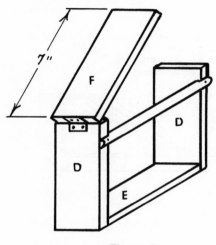

Figure 7

7. Screw the hook and eye into pieces D and G, as shown in Figure 8.

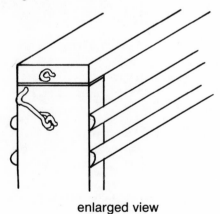

enlarged view

Figure 8

8   Attach assembled pieces D, E and F to piece A with one #8 (¾″ long) round-head wood screw. Stain the feeding station. When you have attached it to a window sill or balcony, fill the suet and birdseed containers and place the filled water dish between the containers.

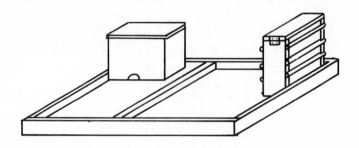

4

Habitats and Equipment
for Amphibians

SALAMANDER TERRARIUM

Salamanders and other amphibians are interesting, inexpensive and decorative creatures. Moreover, they make excellent pets for people who are allergic to fur or feathers. Five varieties of salamanders—spotted, tiger, marbled, dusky and red—do well in captivity. They require a roomy and well-ventilated environment and water in which to submerge themselves. A 5½-gallon, rectangular terrarium with glass sides and a mesh cover will comfortably house one adult salamander approximately eight to ten inches long. A thermometer, affixed to the inside of the terrarium, and an adjustable Dazor lamp, with two full-spectrum, ultraviolet fluorescent tubes, are all that are needed to control the terrarium's climate. The light should be directed toward a spot in the land portion of the terrarium so that the salamander can bask directly beneath the light or crawl into a shady area. Never use bulbs or fluorescent tubes recommended for plant growth. They can be extremely harmful to animals. The terrarium's temperature should always remain between 60° and 70° F.

CONSTRUCTION MATERIALS

5½-gallon rectangular terrarium with glass sides
pane of glass, ⅛" thick (cut to specifications)
aquarium cement (available in pet stores)

FURNISHINGS

adjustable Dazor lamp	humus
2 18" full-spectrum,	small log
ultraviolet fluorescent tubes	twigs, pieces of tree bark
thermometer	and dead leaves
clean, coarse sand	small ferns and mosses
clean gravel, rocks	aquatic plants
and pebbles	water

1. Have a glazier cut a glass divider with a polished edge. It should measure half the height of the terrarium and its inside width.

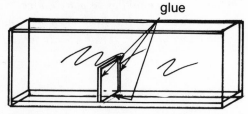

glue

2. Seal the partition in place with aquarium cement. When the cement has dried thoroughly, wash the entire terrarium with soap and hot water.

3. Cover the bottom of each section with a 3″-deep layer of gravel.

4. Plant one of the following in the gravel of the "swimming" section of the terrarium: water lily, vallisneria, elodea, water sprite, sagittaria. Fill the "swimming" section of the terrarium with water you have "aged" for a day or so in a container.

5. Fill the land section with a 3″-deep mixture of equal amounts of sand and rich humus. Using sand, pebbles, gravel, twigs and small rocks, build a slope against the aquatic side of the glass partition so that your salamander can easily climb out of the water onto the land portion of the terrarium.

6. Plant a few small ferns and mosses in the humus-sand mixture and place a small log in the center of the land section. In one corner build a small shelter out of rocks, pebbles, twigs, pieces of tree bark and leaves.

NOTE: The terrarium should be cleaned and the water changed once a week. Never put water straight from a tap into the terrarium. It should first be "aged" in a container since the water's chlorine content can be toxic to amphibians and reptiles. It would be wise to clean the twigs, branches, bark and leaves you place in the terrarium if the materials were once parts of trees that had been sprayed with pesticides. The terrarium should not be placed directly in front of a heating source or in direct sunlight. Keep the plants and the flooring of the land section damp (not soggy) with a daily sprinkling of water.

FROG TERRARIUM

Frogs can be lively and fascinating companions. Heading the list of the most appealing and easiest to keep are: the leopard, gray tree and spring peeper. All three varieties can be kept in the same terrarium if they are more or less the same size. Large frogs have a tendency to become aggressive, and they often attack their smaller relatives. A ten-gallon terrarium makes a suitable living arrangement for four or five medium-sized, adult frogs. Follow the directions for making the salamander terrarium, but make sure that the mesh top of the frog habitat has an escape-proof cover with an attached latch.

TOAD TERRARIUM

The common American toad, or "hop toad," makes a very entertaining pet that sometimes lives as long as thirty years. Contrary to popular belief, toads do not cause warts in humans. But they sometimes emit substances that can be harmful to other animals. A ten-gallon terrarium will house two to three adult toads. They require the same equipment described in the section on habitats and furnishings for salamanders.

5

Habitats and Equipment for Reptiles

LIZARD LOUNGE

Among the many varieties of lizards, the anole (also known as the American chameleon) is the easiest to keep in captivity. Anoles range in size from five to nine inches, and they sometimes change their colors to match their surroundings. The anole thrives in a dry climate, and its habitat can be placed in direct sunlight. But the temperature of the enclosure should always remain between 75° and 80° F. during the daytime and between 65° and 68° F. at night. Water should be lightly sprayed on the sides of an anole's terrarium twice daily. An anole will lap up droplets of water but will usually refuse to drink from a dish. Be sure to "age" the water by placing it in a container for one or two days, since the chlorine content of water drawn directly from a tap can have a toxic effect on anoles.

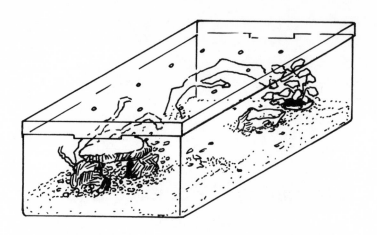

CONSTRUCTION MATERIALS

clear plastic sweater box (with lid), approximately
    11" x 16" x 7"
drill
¼" bit
scrap wood

FURNISHINGS

clean sand and gravel
flat and round rocks
stones, pebbles and twigs
small, branched tree limb
bulb plant spray

gooseneck lamp with 40-watt bulb (optional)

aquatic cement (optional)

small potted artillery fern or Fittonia plant
   (optional)

1. Turn the plastic lid of the sweater box upside down on scrap wood and drill 10 holes, each ¼″ in diameter.

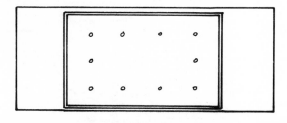

2. Line the bottom of the box with a 2″ mixture of equal amounts of sand and gravel.

3. In one corner of the box make a sheltered sleeping area, large enough to accommodate your anole, with rocks, stones, pebbles and twigs. Make sure the structure is sturdy. If necessary, glue the materials together with aquatic cement.

4. Imbed a small potted plant (preferably a Fittonia or an artillery fern) in the gravel-sand mixture near the shelter, and place a small tree branch in the center of the box.

NOTE: The flooring material should be replaced approximately three times a month, and the terrarium should be thoroughly cleaned at least once a month. If the terrarium is in a location without direct sunlight, substitute a gooseneck lamp with a 40-watt bulb and arrange the lamp so that it shines directly into the terrarium. Never use bulbs or fluorescent tubes recommended for plant growth. They can be extremely harmful to animals.

TORTOISE TERRARIUM

The tortoise, or land turtle, is an attractive and amiable reptile that readily adapts to a life of captivity. If given tender, loving care, the animal's life expectancy ranges from twenty to forty years. A tortoise's basic requirements are few: a vegetarian diet, a light and roomy habitat with a flooring of clean sand, and a small amount of drinking water.

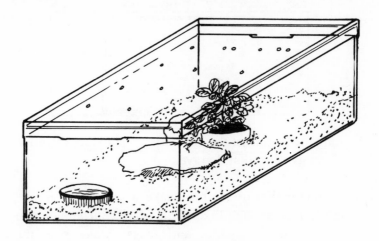

CONSTRUCTION MATERIALS

clear plastic sweater box (with lid), approximately
      11" x 16" x 7"
drill
¼" bit
scrap wood

FURNISHINGS

clean sand
flat rock, approximately 4" in diameter

shallow, plastic or glass drinking dish,
approximately 3″ in diameter
gooseneck lamp with a 40-watt bulb (optional)
small, potted Fittonia or artillery fern (optional)

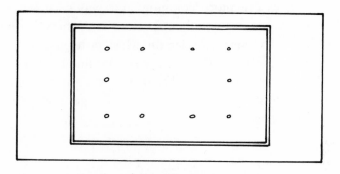

1. Turn the lid of the sweater box upside down on a piece of scrap wood and drill 10 holes in it, each ¼″ in diameter.

2. Place a 2″-deep layer of sand on the bottom of the box and a flat rock in the center of the box. Put a water-filled drinking dish in one corner and a small, potted plant (Fittonia or an artillery fern) near the rock. The terrarium should have equal amounts of sunshine and shade. If necessary, arrange a gooseneck lamp with a 40-watt bulb in such a way that the light shines on only one portion of the terrarium. Never use bulbs or fluorescent tubes recommended for plant growth. They can be extremely harmful to animals.

NOTE: Housing for water turtles, or terrapins, has not been included in this section. Unfortunately, these once-popular pets are no longer sold in pet stores unless the turtles' shells measure over four inches in diameter. The sale of small turtles has been outlawed due to salmonella, a dangerous bacteria carried by small turtles and transmitted to humans and other animals.

SNAKE PIT

The fairly docile garter snake and the California boa are interesting pets that thrive in captivity under proper conditions. Each snake should be caged in a separate habitat.

Garter snakes are more common and better known in North America than any other species. They range from eighteen inches to four feet in length. Most garter snakes live eight to ten years, and as they age, they continue to grow.

Not all boas are large, tropical snakes. The California boa, a small-scale constrictor, makes an attractive pet that grows up to two feet long.

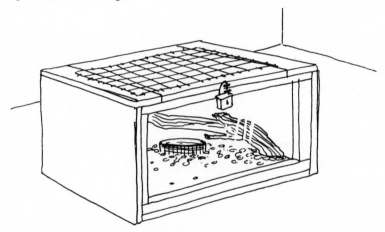

CONSTRUCTION MATERIALS

11½″ x 24″ x ¾″ piece of plywood

2   1″ x 12″ x 18″ pieces of common pine wood
       (actual measurement: ¾″ x 11½″ x 18″)

1″ x 12″ x 22½″ piece of common pine wood
       (actual measurement: ¾″ x 11½″ x 22½″)

1″ x 2″ x 22½″ piece of common pine wood
       (actual measurement: ¾″ x 1⅝″ x 22½″)

2   ¼″ x ⅞″ x 11″ wood lattices

¼″ x ⅞″ x 22″ wood lattice

2   ¾″ x ¾″ baluster moldings, 10″ long

¾″ x ¾″ baluster molding, 21″ long

2   1″ x 3″ x 18¾″ pieces of common pine
wood (actual measurement: ¾″ x 2⅝″ x
18¾″)

2   1″ x 3″ x 19¼″ pieces of common pine
wood (actual measurement: ¾″ x 2⅝″ x
19¼″)

pane of glass, 10¼″ x 22½″ x ⅛″

2   2″ x 1½″ butt hinges

2   ½″ screw eyes

small padlock

17   finishing nails, ¾″ long

17   finishing nails, 1¼″ long

10   finishing nails, 1½″ long

10   #8 flat-head wood screws, 1½″ long

8   #8 flat-head wood screws, ⅝″ long

8   1″ x ¼″ x ⅜″ corrugated nails

hammer   countersink bit

screwdriver   paint brush

crosscut saw   varnish

carpenter's square   sandpaper, medium and fine

staple gun   ruler

drill   pencil

11/64″ bit

FURNISHINGS

litter material or gravel
branched tree limb

91

9″ x 9″ x 2″ aluminum cake pan (for water)

Dazor lamp with 18″ full-spectrum, ultraviolet
    fluorescent tube

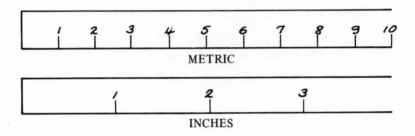

METRIC

INCHES

1. Attach two ¾″ x ¾″ x 10″ baluster moldings to two 1″
   x 12″ x 18″ pieces of wood A and B with ten finishing
   nails, 1¼″ long. Repeat the process with the ¾″ x ¾″
   x 21″ baluster molding and the 1″ x 12″ x 22½″ piece
   of wood C with seven finishing nails 1¼″ long, as
   shown in Figure 1.

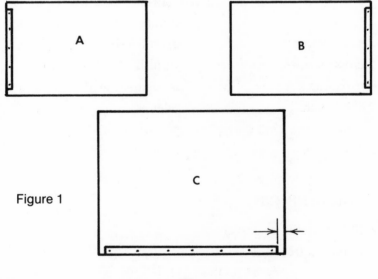

Figure 1

2. Attach two ¼″ x ⅞″ x 11′ lattices to pieces A and B with ten finishing nails, ¾″ long. Measure, mark and drill eight holes with 11/64″ bit at points shown in Figure 2. Countersink the holes on the backs of the pieces.

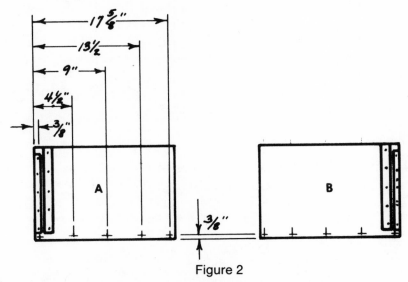

Figure 2

3. Attach the ¼″ x ⅞″ x 22″ lattice to piece C with seven finishing nails, ¾″ long, as shown in Figure 3. Turn piece C upside-down and screw pieces A and B to piece C with eight #8 (1½″ long) flat-head wood screws, as shown in Figure 4.

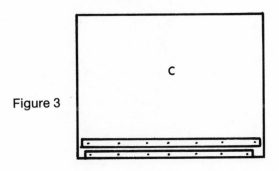

Figure 3

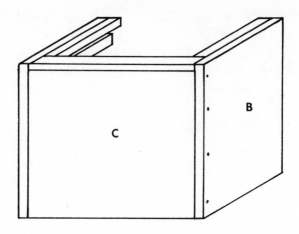

Figure 4

4. Attach the 11½″ x 24″ x ¾″ piece of plywood D to pieces B, C and A with ten finishing nails, 1½″ long, as shown in Figure 5.

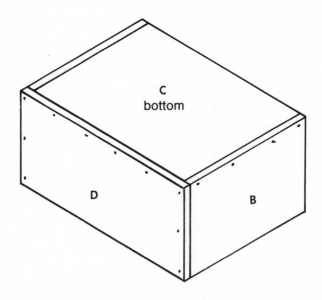

Figure 5

5. Drill two holes in the ¾″ x ¾″ x 21″ baluster molding with 11/64″ bit, as shown in Figure 6. Place the assembled pieces upright and attach the baluster molding with two #8 (1½″ long) flat-head wood screws, to pieces A and B.

Screw ¾″ × ¾″ × 22″ baluster molding here.

lattice

A

baluster
molding

Figure 6

95

6. Place two 1″ x 3″ x 18¾″ pieces of wood E and F and two 1″ x 3″ x 19¼″ pieces of wood G and H on a level surface. Hammer them to each other with corrugated nails, as shown in Figure 7.

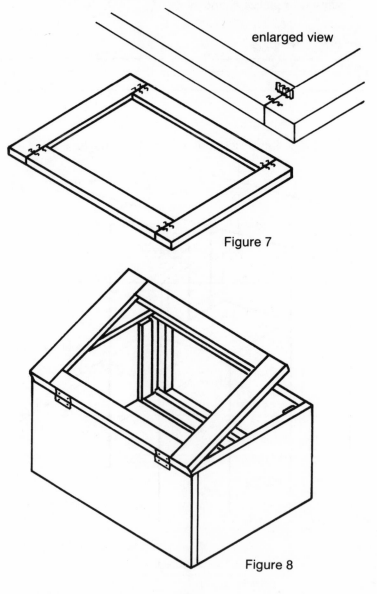

enlarged view

Figure 7

Figure 8

7. Place assembled pieces E, F, G and H on top of the box. On the back edge of the lid attach one side of each hinge with four #8 (⅝" long) flat-head wood screws. Screw the other parts of the hinges to the back of the box with four #8 (⅝" long) flat-head wood screws, as shown in Figure 8.

8. Center the hardware cloth over the opening on the lid and staple it to the wood. Attach two screw eyes to the center of the lid, as shown in Figure 9.

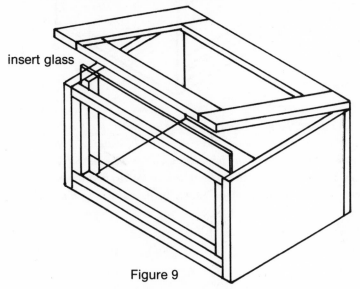

insert glass

Figure 9

Sand the wood and varnish it. When thoroughly dry, insert the pane of glass into the slot. To lock the lid, place the padlock through the screw eyes. Place litter material or gravel on the bottom of the box. Smooth the branched tree limb with sandpaper.

NOTE: A snake's water container should be large enough for complete immersion. Snakes must soak in water in order to shed their skins. Wedge the tree limb in one corner of the cage. Place the water container away from the glass side because snakes usually like to

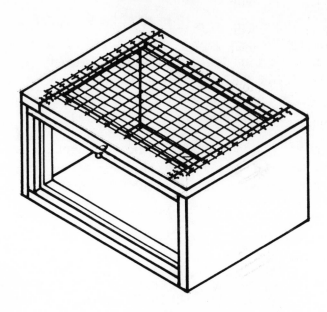

stretch out along the glass. Slope the flooring material near the water container so that the snake has easy access to the water. A gooseneck lamp with a 40-watt bulb may be substituted for the adjustable Dazor lamp with a fluorescent tube. Never use bulbs or fluorescent tubes recommended for plant growth. They can be extremely harmful to animals.

6

Habitats and Equipment for Insects

ANT FARM

Ants and their fascinating behavior have been objects of study throughout the centuries. Most of the species can be kept easily and very inexpensively. If an ant colony is housed in a glass-sided habitat, you can observe them tunneling in the earth, transporting food and carrying out other activities. A sponge, kept wet and placed on the surface of the soil, will provide the necessary amount of moisture for the colony.

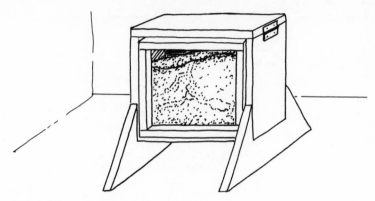

CONSTRUCTION MATERIALS

12″ x 13″ x ¾″ piece of plywood

1   ¼″ x ⅞″ x 11″ wood lattice

2   ¼″ x ⅞″ x 10¼″ wood lattices

2   ¾″ x ¾″ baluster moldings, 11½″ long

2   ¾″ x ¾″ baluster moldings, 9″ long

2   1″ x 2″ x 13″ pieces of common pine wood
(actual measurement: ¾″ x 1⅝″ x 13″)

2   1″ x 2″ x 10½″ pieces of common pine
wood (actual measurement: ¾″ x 1⅝″ x 10½″)

pane of glass, 10½″ x 11½″ x ⅛″

1½″ x 1″ butt hinge

4   #6 flat-head wood screws, ¾″ long

4   #8 flat-head wood screws, 1½″ long

2   #8 flat-head wood screws, 1¼″ long

1″ hook and eye

24   finishing nails, ¾″ long

23   finishing nails, 1¼″ long

10   finishing nails, 1½″ long

crosscut saw   countersinking bit

hammer   fine sandpaper

screwdriver   paint brush
drill   pencil
½″ bit   ruler
11/64″ bit   shellac or varnish

FURNISHINGS

garden soil
small sponge

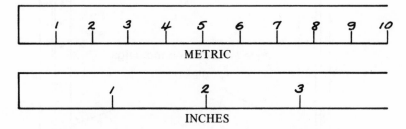

1. With fourteen finishing nails, ¾″ long, attach the ¼″ x
   ⅞″ x 11″ lattice to 1″ x 2″ x 13″ piece of wood B.
   With ten finishing nails, ¾″ long, attach two ¼″ x ⅞″
   x 10¼″ lattices to two 1″ x 2″ x 10½″ pieces of wood
   C and D, as shown in Figure 1.

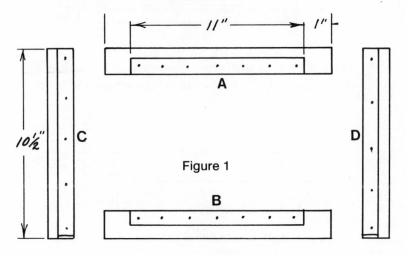

Figure 1

2. Attach the two ¾″ x ¾″ x 9″ baluster moldings to pieces C and D with ten finishing nails, 1¼″ long, as shown in Figure 2. Attach one of the ¾″ x ¾″ x 11½″ baluster molding to piece B with seven finishing nails, 1¼″ long.

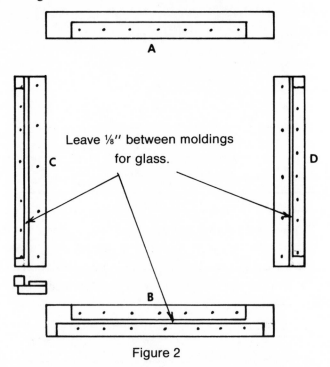

Figure 2

3. Turn piece B upside down. Measure, mark and drill four holes with the 11/64″ bit. Countersink the holes, as shown in Figure 3.

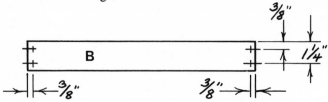

Figure 3

4. Screw piece B to pieces C and D with four #8 (1½″ long) flat-head wood screws, as shown in Figure 4. Drill two holes into the other ¾″ x ¾″ x 11½″ baluster molding. Attach with 2 #8 (1¼″ long) flat-head wood screws, as shown in Figure 4. Attach piece E to pieces B, C and D with ten finishing nails, 1½″ long, as shown in Figure 5.

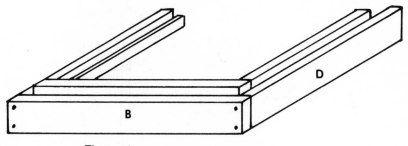

Figure 4

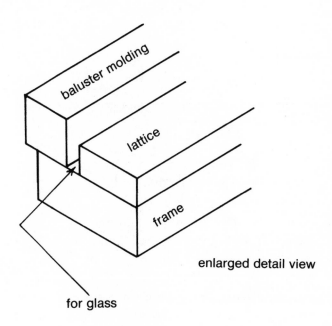

enlarged detail view

for glass

Figure 5

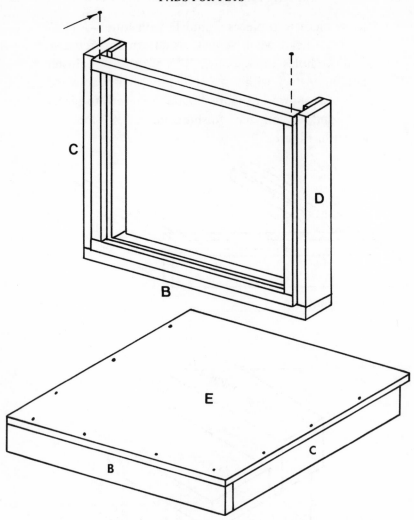

5. Center the butt hinge on the end of piece A and attach it with two #8 (¾″ long) flat-head wood screws, as shown in Figure 6. Place piece A on top of pieces C and D and attach the other part of the hinge to the side of piece D with two #8 (¾″ long) flat-head wood screws, as shown in Figure 7. Screw the hook and eye in position to piece A and the side of

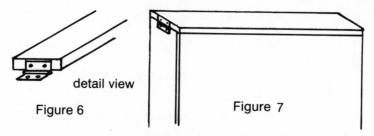

detail view

Figure 6

Figure 7

piece C, as shown in Figure 8. Sand the wood and varnish and shellac it. When the wood has thoroughly dried, insert the pane of glass between the two moldings, as shown in Figure 9. Fill the enclosure with soil, leaving a two-inch space at the top. Moisten the sponge and place it on top of the soil.

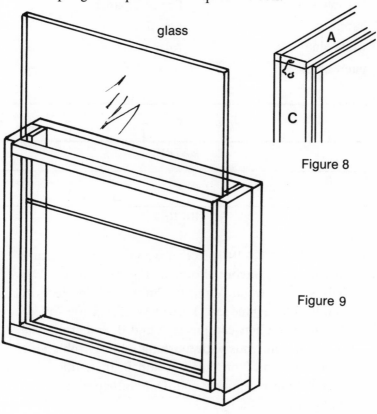

glass

A

C

Figure 8

Figure 9

CONSTRUCTION MATERIALS FOR
AN ANT FARM STAND

1   1″ x 8″ x 10″ piece of common pine wood
(actual measurement: ¾″ x 7½″ x 10″)

1   ½″ x 2″ x 12″ piece of common pine wood
(actual measurement: ½″ x 1½″ x 12″)

1   ½″ x 2″ x 10½″ piece of common pine
wood

4   finishing nails, 1¼″ long

crosscut saw   paint or stain
keyhole saw   fine sandpaper
hammer   pencil
white glue   ruler
paint brush

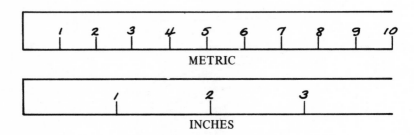

1. Saw a 1″ x 8″ x 10″ piece of wood in half. Measure
and draw the layout shown in Figure 1 on the two
halves of the wood A and B. Cut notches in pieces A
and B with keyhole saw. Insert a ½″ x 2″ x 10½″ piece
of pine wood between pieces A and B, and attach the
pieces at both ends with finishing nails. Dribble glue
at points 1 and 2 on pieces A and B. Insert the ½″ x
2″ x 12″ piece of pine wood, D. Sandpaper the wood
and paint or stain it.

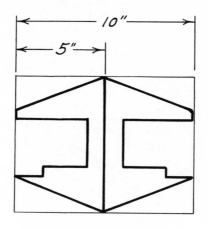

Figure 1

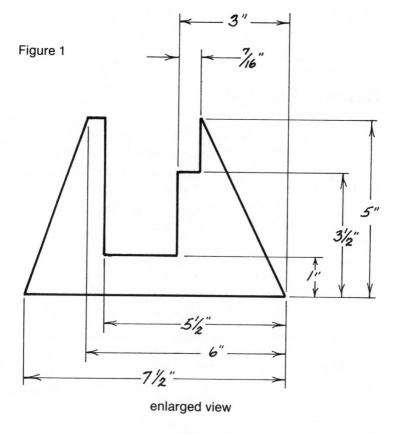

enlarged view

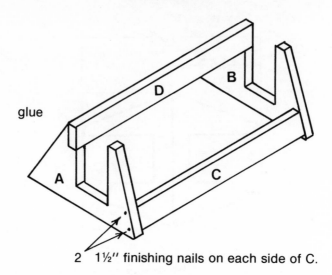

glue

2   1½″ finishing nails on each side of C.

CRICKET CASTLE

Crickets are just as simple to keep as ants. The male crickets make cheerful noises by rubbing their wings together, but there should be only one male to a cricket habitat because male crickets fight with one another. Crickets need a constant supply of water which can be provided by placing a wet sponge in a small glass dish (the kind used for moistening postage stamps) on top of the habitat's sand flooring.

CONSTRUCTION MATERIALS

5-lb. glass food container with screw lid
drill
¼″ bit

FURNISHINGS

clean sand
small, flat stones
small sponge and glass dish
twig

1. Drill 8 holes in the glass container's lid.

2. Place a 2″ layer of sand on the bottom of the container. Add stones, a twig and a moistened sponge in its glass container.

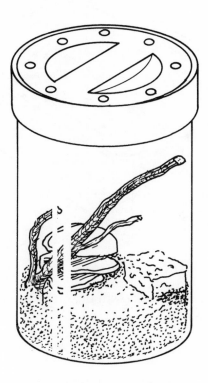

TARANTULA TERRARIUM

The fact that tarantulas are not really insects at all may come as a surprise to many people. Tarantulas and other spiders are arachnids, relatives of horseshoe crabs and scorpions. Despite the tarantula's notorious reputation, its bite is no more dangerous than the sting of a honeybee; it is relatively harmless to most humans. As with ants, crickets and other insects, tarantulas do well in a moist, covered habitat. Water should be sprayed on to the sides of the enclosure or served in a small, shallow dish, approximately 3″ in diameter.

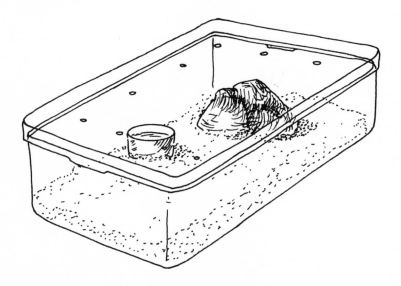

CONSTRUCTION MATERIALS

clear plastic sweater box (with lid), approximately
    11″ x 16″ x 7″
drill
¼″ bit
scrap wood

FURNISHINGS

clean gravel
clean sand
flat rock
water dish
plant bulb spray (optional)

1. Turn the lid of the sweater box upside down on scrap wood and drill 10 holes, ¼″ in diameter, as shown in Figure 1.

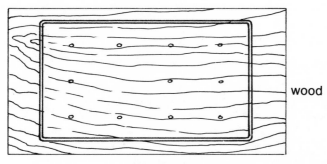

wood

Figure 1

2. Put a 2″-deep mixture of equal amounts of sand and gravel on the bottom of the box. Add a rock and a water dish.

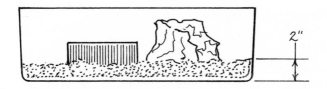

2″

NOTE: A tarantula's terrarium should be kept at room temperature, away from sunlight and radiators or other heating devices.

Common Metric Equivalents and Conversions

APPROXIMATE

1 inch	= 25 millimeters
1 foot	= 0.3 meter
1 yard	= 0.9 meter
1 square inch	= 6.5 square centimeters
1 square foot	= 0.09 square meter
1 square yard	= 0.8 square meter
1 millimeter	= 0.04 inch
1 meter	= 3.3 feet
1 meter	= 1.1 yards
1 square centimeter	= 0.16 square inch

ACCURATE TO PARTS PER MILLION

inches x 25.4	= millimeters
feet x 0.3048	= meters
yards x 0.9144	= meters
square inches x 6.4516	= square centimeters
square feet x 0.092903	= square meters
square yards x 0.836127	= square meters

TEMPERATURE CONVERSION

The Celsius scale (C), often called the centigrade scale, is derived from the Fahrenheit scale by the following formula:

$$C = \frac{5\,(F-32)}{9}$$

Bibliography

Boy Scouts of America. *Veterinary Science.* New Brunswick, N.J., 1973.

Christopher, William Miller, and West, Geoffrey P. *Encyclopedia of Animal Care.* Baltimore: Williams and Wilkins, 1964.

Dennis, John V. *A Complete Guide to Bird Feeding.* New York: Knopf, 1975.

Forshaw, Joseph M. *Parrots of the World.* New York: Doubleday, 1973.

Guthrie, Esther L. *Home Book of Animal Care.* New York: Harper, 1966.

Headstrom, Richard. *Frogs, Toads, and Salamanders as Pets.* New York: McKay, 1972.

———.*Your Insect Pet.* New York: McKay, 1973.

Leedham, Charles. *Care of the Dog.* New York: Scribner's, 1961.

Low, Rosemary. *Aviary Birds.* South Brunswick, N.J.: A. S. Barnes, 1970.

McDonald, Peter. *Animal Nutrition.* New York: Hafner, 1973.

Peterson, Roger Tory. *A Field Guide to the Birds.* Boston: Houghton Mifflin, 1969.

Pillsbury, Ernest W. *First Aid and Care of Small Animals.* New York: New York Animal Welfare Institute, 1955.

Terres, John K. *Songbirds in Your Garden.* New York: Crowell, 1968.

Villard, Paul. *Birds as Pets.* Garden City: Doubleday, 1974.

Whitney, Leon. *Pets.* New York: McKay, 1971.

Index